INNOVATIONS IN EDUCATING COMMUNITIES
ABOUT LEARNING DISABILITIES

THE
MENTAL
HEALTH

FOUNDATION

and

Lisieux Hall Publications

Innovations in Educating Communities about
Learning Disabilities

Published by: Lisieux Hall, Whittle-le-Woods, Chorley, Lancashire, England, PR6 7DX

in association with

Mental Health Foundation, 37 Mortimer Street, London W1N 7RJ

A catalogue entry for this book is available from the British Library

ISBN 1-870335-14-7

Dedication

In August 1944, two Brothers of Charity, came to Gorebridge on the outskirts of Edinburgh, to start up a community in which the Brothers would share their lives with people who in those days were known as 'mental defectives'.

Fifty years on, their work continues in Borders Region of Scotland, albeit in a very different form but with the same intention that everyone, no matter how severe their disability, needs to be part of a community.

This book marks the golden jubilee of the Congregation's work in Scotland and is dedicated to the Brothers who down through the years have contributed to making community life more of a reality for Scots folk with learning disabilities.

Innovations in Educating Communities about Learning Disabilities

Edited by

Roy McConkey

Lisieux Hall Publications, Chorley, Lancashire in association with the Mental Health Foundation, London

Other Publications available from Lisieux Hall

Innovations in Educating Children with Severe Learning Disabilities
edited by John Harris, (£9 + £1.50 p&p)
> *It is rare to read a book about the national curriculum and children with severe learning disabilities that is readable and practical. But this is one such book* Care Weekly

Innovations in Employment Training and Work for People with Learning Difficulties edited by Roy McConkey & Patrick McGinley (£9 + £1.50 p&p)
> *...useful practical guide to a number of innovative programmes in vocational training and employment in the UK and other countries.* Mental Handicap Research

Innovations in Leisure and Recreation for People with a Mental Handicap edited by Roy McConkey & Patrick McGinley (£9+£1.50 p&p)
> *...practical and enthusiastic .. can be highly recommended not only to practitioners in the field but to all those wishing to become involved in leisure activities for people with a mental handicap.* International Journal of Rehabilitation Research

Innovations in Family Support for People with Disabilities edited by Peter and Helle Mittler (£9 + £1.50 p&p)
> *This book sets out in an easy-to-read format, a range of innovative projects described so that other service-providers can replicate them. Topics covered include: family rights; home visiting services; school-based support; family-based respite care; supporting siblings; working with ethnic minorities and help for aging carers.*

Going Places with Volunteers - Creating an Enabling Community Environment edited by Brian Kelly (£3 + £1.50 p&p)
> *Examines an important aspect of social integration ... written in a clear, useable form .. a positive agenda for recreational opportunities confirming the mutual benefits of such a scheme.* Mencap News

Mental Handicap: Challenge to the Church edited by Brian Kelly and Patrick McGinley (£9 + £1.50 p&p)
> *...gives helpful advice and encouragement ... opens out new possibilities and insights to all who are involved in the challenge the Church faces in the care of the mentally handicapped.* Life and Work (Church of Scotland)

Innovations in Educating Communities about Learning Disabilities

CONTENTS

SECTION 3: TIPS AND TECHNIQUES

SECTION 4: RESOURCES FOR EDUCATING COMMUNITIES

FOREWORD

The hostile reactions of many neighbourhoods to the establishment of local facilities for people with special needs has given a new word to the English language - NIMBYISM - *Not In My BackYard!*

This unattractive manifestation of fear of the unknown; of ignorance of those of us who are different from the rest of us, takes many forms - from protest meetings, to petitions and media campaigns, and even the harassment and ostracising of eventual service users.

But is it just that human beings are inevitably and fundamentally selfish, narrow and prejudiced, or is there something which the planners and providers of services could do to harness the energy in a positive rather than negative way?

Roy McConkey has drawn together the experience and wisdom of a wide range of people - people with learning disabilities, carers, teachers, nurses and other providers of services - attending a series of workshops to look at how communities can be enabled to include people with learning disabilities into ordinary, day-to-day life.

The workshops were all held in Scotland and they focused specifically on the needs of people with learning disabilities but the overall message of the book could apply just as readily to other people who do not fit general preconceptions of what is normal, for example, those with physical disabilities or mental health problems. It could also apply to any part of the UK or for that matter, the western world.

This is essentially a recipe book, describing the ingredients and methods necessary to build richer, healthier, more open and more balanced communities. Places we would all find it more pleasant to live in.

June McKerrow
Director: Mental Health Foundation

Roy McConkey

Roy McConkey is Director of Training and Research with the Brothers of Charity Services in the Borders Region of Scotland; a voluntary organisation providing community residential and day training services to 130 men and women with learning disabilities.

A native of Belfast and a psychologist by training, he has previously worked with St. Michael's House, Dublin and at the Hester Adrian Research Centre, University of Manchester.

He is a member of the Learning Disabilities Committee of the Mental Health Foundation and from 1991-1994, directed the Educating Communities Network in Scotland funded by the Foundation.

He is the author or co-author of nine books in the field of special needs and with Patrick McGinley has edited two further books in the present series - *Innovations in Leisure and Recreation* and *Innovations in Employment Training and Work*.

PREFACE

This book is the product of many people. In 1991, the Mental Health Foundation sponsored the formation within Scotland of an Educating Communities Network. The main aim was to foster local initiatives at making communities more aware of the needs of people who have learning disabilities and to promote their inclusion in ordinary community activities.

This 'grass-roots' approach necessitated the active involvement of local people, be they professional workers, family carers, community workers, volunteer helpers or persons with a disability. The Network provided a means for over 150 Scots to connect with like-minded people and more crucially, offered opportunities to empower each other with the knowledge and skills required to undertake this task.

One of the Network's core activities was a series of eleven, one-day training workshops. Six workshops were centred around a specific target group from the community - schools, employers, media, politicians, neighbours and churches - and a further five dealt with specific techniques such as conducting surveys, finding volunteers, using video, involving people with profound disabilities and evaluating the impact of community initiatives.

Each workshop was led by an invited guest who had particular experience of the topic. In addition, one or more members of the network gave an account of their experiences in Scotland. Key issues were then discussed by all workshop participants. Their advice and recommendations were then collated and made available to Network members through a series of booklets.

This book brings together for a wider readership the wisdom and experiences of ordinary folk throughout Scotland and beyond, about how best local communities can be educated about disability.

This is no academic treatise or wishful thinking. Rather it is the 'down-to-earth' advice of colleagues who have ventured ahead of us and from whose mistakes and achievements we can learn.

The book will be a resource to individuals who are already engaged in community work or who are about to embark upon it. But the book is also aimed at a wider and much larger audience; the many thousands of professional workers, carers and people with a disability who proclaim the need for communities to be educated but who do little or nothing to contribute to the task.

Nor will reading a book convert them to action. Rather, as the canny Scot, Thomas Carlyle observed, *there can be no acting or doing of any kind, till it be recognized that there is a thing to be done. The thing once recognized, doing in a thousand shapes become possible.* The failure to recognise takes various forms.

☐ We fail to acknowledge that people with learning disabilities, no matter how severe, have a right to live within ordinary communities and will benefit from so doing.

☐ We fail to realise that the majority of people within local communities are welcoming but seek advice on how they should react to people they perceive as different to themselves.

☐ We fail to appreciate that the most effective community education involves creating relationships among people rather than giving information.

These failures can be tackled in many different contexts - reviews of individual's needs; staff meetings and advocacy groups. But in all the common starting point is the needs of the person with a disability. Once these are recognised, then, as this book amply illustrates,'doing in a thousand shapes' becomes possible.

ACKNOWLEDGEMENTS

Books, like television shows, may have one presenter but the production is only possible because of the team behind the scenes. I am happy to give credit and thanks to:

♦ The Mental Health Foundation for sponsoring the Network and co-publishing the book;

♦ The Network members throughout Scotland who willing shared their expertise and experiences;

♦ My employers, the Brothers of Charity, who made it possible for me to undertake this work;

♦ The invited speakers and participants in all the workshops who are named throughout the book;

♦ My colleagues, Brian Kelly and Patrick McGinley at Lisieux Hall Publications for their helpful suggestions;

♦ Lisa McGill for the cartoons;

and most importantly,

♦ The staff and users in our services in Borders Region Scotland who constantly remind me of the needs of people with learning disabilities and the continuing challenge we all face.

WHAT'S IN A NAME?

People who in Britain today are labelled as having a 'learning disability' have been called many other names; such as *mentally handicapped* and *mentally subnormal* to name but two. Internationally a range of labels are used, including *mentally retarded* and *intellectually disabled*. Colloquially a myriad of labels have evolved over the years; for instance *simple, wee want* and *not the full shilling*.

Emotive debates have raged among, and between, professionals, families and self-advocates about the choice of names for this disability. The label is crucial for anyone embarking on any form of community education and involvement yet there is no easy solution to the dilemmas posed by the apparently simple choice of name.

Labels stereotype ....

Terms such as *'mental'* conjure up images of people with bizarre behaviours and *'handicap'* of people in wheelchairs. Not surprising, people resent being stereotyped. Hence many self-advocates do not want to be known as 'mentally handicapped' preferring a term such as *person with learning difficulties* or *slow learner*

... but labels identify Groups of people in our society have special needs. We use labels to identify such groupings and to distinguish them from each other; for instance according to their disability. The needs of people with a physical disability are different from those with a visual impairment or a learning disability. Labels are unavoidable when we want to promote the rights and needs of a section of our community. Moreover the terms chosen must be precise and capable of conveying the seriousness of their needs. The word *disability* is preferable to *difficulties*.

Labels can devalue ...

Prejudices are easily conveyed through choice of words. Many labels for people with disabilities have become terms of abuse - *idiot, mongol, spastic,* A similar fate may await any new label invented to replace older words. The solution, some argue, is to avoid generic labels and to be specific; for example, using an individual's name - *Paul and Mary both need a job* rather than 'people with learning disabilities need jobs'; or the term *Down's syndrome* to 'mongol'.

.... but labels can also promote

Labels can bring together people with a common cause and unite them in a common purpose, such as has happened with gay rights and black Americans. Similar moves are afoot among people with physical and sensorial impairments who urge others to take 'pride' in their disability. Advocates of this approach prefer terms which are up-front; for example preferring *'disabled'* to *'special needs'*. In this way, their needs for extra help and positive discrimination are then emphasised. Likewise a common humanity is emphasised by referring first to the person rather than the disability, e.g. *teenagers with Down's syndrome; Glaswegians with epilepsy.*

Labels can deceive

In the sense that the labels invariably focus attention on the problem being the disability when in reality the problem is more likely to be the handicaps which arise from the disability and the way our society responds to these. For example, people who are unable to walk would be less handicapped if our footpaths, buildings and public transport were easily accessible for wheelchair users.

Such thinking is even more apposite for the condition known internationally as 'intellectual disabilities'. The phrase implies a common bodily impairment when in reality it is nothing more than an umbrella term for a host of diverse conditions some with biological origins while others stem from social causes.

Common needs rather than common causes typify this disability which prompted Marc Gold to redefine 'mentally retarded people' as those who require *above average training procedures and superior adaptive functioning from society*; thereby emphasising a more accurate focus as to where their problems lie. A similar notion underlies the use of the phrase 'labelled as' in my opening sentence: *people labelled as having a learning disability* or the expressions *clients of our service* or *service-users*.

Building new images of disability

Image, as any public relations consultant will tell you, is crucial. However the images conjured up by the older labels listed above are likely to be counter-productive to community involvement. Yet it is by these very names that the wider public knows of whom we are talking.

Breaking this cycle requires more than a change of name, although that too is probably necessary. Rather new images and associations have to be built in people's minds. This is best done by:

☐ **personal contacts:** opportunities to meet and talk with individuals from the group of labelled people. The image we need to promote is of ordinary people coping successfully with disability and NOT the work of special services no matter how worthy they are.

☐ **stressing personal attributes:** such as sense of humour, talent for singing; memory for names; swimming prowess, manual dexterity and so on. This should balance the "can't do" image that disability labels perpetuate.

☐ **emphasising needs:** equally by emphasising a need for employment or for more choice of leisure pursuits, we spotlight their common humanity and the responses which local people can make.

☐ **correcting misinformation:** among the most common is confusion about mental illness and learning disability, and the risks from physical and sexual attacks. Dialogue with local groups is the only sure way of determining their concerns. Clear, concise and honest answers need to be given, preferably verbally so that people have a chance to ask further questions.

☐ **understanding why:** last, but also hardest of all, is to get people thinking about the complexity of relationships within our society; an individual's rights and responsibilities and the values which we as individuals or communities cherish. Past experience suggests that this is likely to be a protracted process and one which is rarely completed.

A change of name?

Changing group labels can be quickly fixed and may be politically correct but unless accompanied by a process of re-education all the old negative images will soon transfer to the new label and another change will be required. A wiser strategy, I suspect is to help people build new images of these people and then new names will be found and adopted.

This means first using the names by which local people refer to these people but as our contacts develop, introducing and explaining the terms favoured locally by the people with the disability and their advocates. Human language is infinitely inventive and although at times it is essential to have universal agreement on a single label (as in legal documents) , most times we can still communicate comfortably and effectively by having various terms for the same referent. Just think of the numbers of words used to refer to 'toilet' for instance. Equal tolerance should be shown for the various terms chosen or created locally to refer to people now labelled as having a learning disability rather than insisting that one phrase is more correct than another.

Indeed, the term *learning disability* is used throughout the book, not because it is the best available - which it isn't - but simply because of its increasing usage in Britain. Please substitute your preferred term, or better still none at all, if you can keep in mind all the individuals from whom local communities are likely to shy away.

SECTION 1
A STRATEGY FOR EDUCATING COMMUNITIES

Educating communities is a multi-facet task which never ends. It cannot be delegated to one or two individuals as a special project or vaguely assigned as someone else's responsibility. Yet these are the two most common responses to this endeavour along with the naive belief that a national television and press advertising campaign is THE solution ... if only the money was available!

In this section a strategy is outlined for educating communities which embraces all the 'stake-holders' - people with disability; family carers; professional workers; service providers and politicians - and makes the task everyone's responsibility while recognising that the various players can contribute in different ways according to their opportunities and talents. The same strategy could be usefully applied to educate the wider public about other marginalised groups; whether with a disability or not.

The strategy is described in the final part of the section and the rationale for it is outlined in four earlier parts. Information collected through the Educating Communities Network is presented, particularly data collected from individual interviews with nearly 1,000 members of the public. The views of people with learning disabilities about educating communities are also summarised.

The five parts in this section are:

☐ Why Bother Educating Communities?

☐ Perceptions of 'Mental Handicap' in
Scottish Communities.

☐ Changing Attitudes - What Works?

☐ The Views of People with Learning Disabilities

☐ A Strategy for Educating Communities

WHY BOTHER EDUCATING COMMUNITIES?

The tasks involved in educating communities about disability can demand a great deal of time and energy. They may also result in disappointment and disagreements, which saps motivation and causes people to give up trying. Hence the rationale for undertaking this work must be clearly thought out and debated with all interested stake-holders. From this, decisions about priorities and methods can be made more easily as will the arguments for the necessary resources to undertake the job.

Obviously a detailed rationale will vary across communities but it is likely that some or all of the following reasons will feature.

The rights of children and adults with disabilities

International declarations of rights invariably mention the right to 'full participation and equality'; to use the slogan from the International Year of Disabled People in 1981. Often this is spelt out in some detail; most recently in the 1990 Convention of Rights of the Child.

> *State Parties recognize that a mentally or physically disabled child should enjoy a full and decent life, in conditions which ensure dignity, promote self-reliance and facilitate the child's active participation in the community.*

Yet many policy-makers still ignore or deny these rights.

'Ordinary life' services

The dominant philosophy in modern services for people with learning disabilities is that they are based on the principles of ordinary living; namely that people's special needs are met as far as possible in ordinary settings. Hence the increased numbers of children in mainstream schools; the many adults who now live in ordinary housing schemes and the growing number in open

employment.   Community care is slowly becoming a reality.
These new styles of services can be jeopardised by an uninformed
and unsympathetic response from the local people involved in
these settings.

Quality of life

In the past, many people with a learning disability were confined
to an institutional existence in which their basic needs were met
but little else was offered; hardly the recipe for a fulfilled life.
Quality of life comes from the opportunities, activities and
relationships open to us.   Specialist services, no matter how well
resourced, can ever replicate what local communities have created
for themselves.   By participating in these communities we can
ensure a better quality of life for people with disabilities but this
can only come about through the active participation of everyone
in that community.

Help and support

Arguably the greatest need of people with a learning disability is
for people to help and support them with tasks which they find
difficult to do on their own.   Often specialist expertise is not
required to do this and anyway, the help and support often needs
to be provided in the context of ordinary community activities
rather than confined to specialist centre.   The solution then is to
enlist the help of local people, usually in a volunteer capacity, to
provide such assistance.

Hence workmates provide the extra 'coaching' which a young lady
with Down's Syndrome might need when she first starts working
in a local supermarket.   Or a member of the photographic club
agrees to call in his car at the group home to bring one of the
residents, John, to club meetings.

The goodwill that undoubtedly exists in most communities cannot be tapped unless an effort is made to make people aware of other's needs and how they can help. Educating communities should result in greater opportunities for involvement and integration.

Aspirations of people with disabilities

Although last, this is arguably the most important reason. Many of our existing services for people with disabilities and their families are still pervaded by old notions of charity - 'take what you are given and count yourself lucky'. With increasing emphasis on empowering the 'consumer' and the encouragement of advocacy such attitudes will become part of our social history. Instead, services will have to attune themselves to the needs and aspirations of their clients. Already the evidence is overwhelming that these children and adults want the same choices and opportunities as their able-bodied peers.

Building an inclusive society means reducing the perceived differences between the labelled minorities and the majority. Years of social conditioning and separation have blinded the so-called able-bodied to the common humanity they share with those deemed to be disabled.

Ensuring that people with disabilities are included in all aspects of community life will break down the barriers but experience has shown that this can be counter-productive if people's legitimate concerns are not addressed and appropriate encouragement given. Educating communities is therefore ultimately about fulfilling the aspirations of people with a disability to live the life of an ordinary citizen.

Further Reading

Audit Commission (1989). *Developing community care for adults with a mental handicap,* London, HMSO.

Fraser, W.I. *et al* (1991). *Hallas' caring for people with mental handicap: Eighth edition,* Oxford, Butterworth-Heinemann.

Mental Health Foundation (1993). *Learning Disability - the Fundamental Facts,* London, Mental Health Foundation.

Scottish Health Service Advisory Council (1992). *The future of mental handicap hospital services in Scotland,* Edinburgh, HMSO.

Shearer, A. (1986). *Building Community - People with mental handicaps, their families and friends,* London, King's Fund Centre.

Towell, D. (ed.) (1988). *An ordinary life in practice: Developing community based services for people with learning disabilities,* London, King's Fund Centre.

PERCEPTIONS OF 'MENTAL HANDICAP' IN SCOTTISH COMMUNITIES

Effective education has to start with each community's present perceptions and preoccupations. As part of the Educating Communities Network various surveys were undertaken with specific communities from different areas - Glasgow, Borders and Dundee - and from different backgrounds - shopkeepers, employers and neighbours. This data was supplemented with information from a research project sponsored by the Scottish Home and Health Department and carried out with residents of housing estates in Central Region. (Fuller reports of each survey are available and they are listed below.)

The information was collected mainly through face-to-face interviews. This approach is much more informative than written questionnaires but it is time-consuming, labour intensive and can be costly. However the network members obtained their information at relatively low cost by using a range of interviewers, including students on service placements, volunteers recruited and trained specifically for the task and the staff and service users from a resource centre for adult persons with learning disabilities. A later section contains tips and advice on carrying out similar surveys (see p. 209).

In all, 992 people took part in all the surveys and in this section, we summarise their common perceptions of mental handicap. These are grouped as follows:

* Contact with people labelled as 'mentally handicapped'
* Concerns and potential problems
* Supporting people in the community.

Incidentally the label *mental handicap* was used in most of the surveys as past studies suggest that this is the term which is best understood by the general public.

Survey Reports

Attitudes to People with Learning Disabilities in seven
Urban Priority Areas of Glasgow
Joan Storrie, Stewart Robinson, Penny Forshaw
and Roy McConkey

The Neighbours Project: Reactions of neighbours and
shopkeepers in the vicinity of a Resource Centre in Dundee.
Pamela Robbie, Cathy Barclay, Christine Fisher, Graeme Millar,
Sheila Gorrie, Craig Mullay, Bill Reekie, Billy Dockery
and Julie Ridley

Reactions of shopkeepers and services in a Scottish Town
to people with learning difficulties.
Roy McConkey and Deirdre Barron

Employers' attitudes to people with learning difficulties:
Contrasts between those with experience and those without
Gloria Hanna and Roy McConkey

Community attitudes and the willingness to 'care' for people
with mental handicaps. Comparisons among four areas in
Central Region with different residential facilities and one with
no resource.
Sally Cheseldine, Paul Dickens and Janine Robinson
Funded by grant from Scottish Home and Health Department

Copies of each report are available free of charge from:
Educating Communities Network
St Aidan's
Gattonside
Melrose TD6 9NN
Borders, Scotland

Contact with people labelled as 'mentally handicapped'

Only a minority of people have had personal contact with people who have a mental handicap. In Glasgow and Dundee, for example, only one in five of people living in housing schemes reported 'regular' contact; whereas nearly three out of five had no contact.

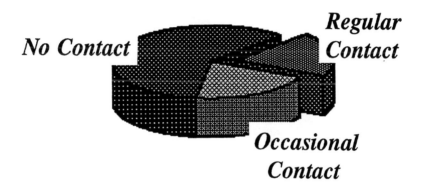

The contacts came in a variety of ways; through ordinary daily activities such as shopping, in the course of their work, when walking around the neighbourhood, or they had relatives with the disability.

For people living in the vicinity of service facilities the contact was naturally higher. This was greatest for neighbours living in the vicinity of a large mental handicap hospital; nearly all of whom reported regular contact but community contacts was lower for small group homes. Typically only around half of the neighbours and local shop-keepers reported contact with residents.

However a much smaller proportion are likely to know any of the local people by name. In a Border town for example, only one quarter of the shop-keepers who recognised the customers from the group home knew their name.

Awareness of services

Linked with this issue, is the local community's awareness of services and what they offer. People living close to a large mental handicap hospital are obviously aware of its existence but the survey in that vicinity discovered that only half of the people could accurately locate and name it. Around one quarter confused it with a nearby psychiatric hospital.

One third of the neighbours of a large resource centre in Dundee were unaware of its existence; only half knew it was a centre for persons with 'learning disabilities' and at best only one in five could say what sort of activities were carried out in the centre.

Groups home located in community settings are likely to be known by around 50% of their neighbours.

In general, the public's contact with services is minimal. In Glasgow, for example only 21 out of 355 people (7%) had ever had any contact with a service for people with 'mental handicap'. Usually this took the form of being given information or an invitation to an Open Day. No one had actually visited a day centre or residence. But then very few of the neighbours living beside centres or homes have been inside them. For example, only eight out of 110 neighbours of the Dundee Centre had visited on an Open Day or to see a friend or relative.

Implications

● *The majority of people have had no personal contact with people who have learning disabilities. Hence their images are likely to be stereotyped and possibly mistaken.*

● *Locating people with disabilities in community settings is no guarantee that they will meet and get to know local people. Introductions need to be made and opportunities provided for acquaintances to be forged.*

● *Public awareness is minimal as regards the aims, style and content of services provided for people with learning disabilities. They likely harbour outmoded ideas which in turn reinforces their stereotyped images of these people.*

● *Most worrying of all is the public's lack of involvement or contact with facilities within their own neighbourhood. In what sense can we talk about these as being **community** facilities if local people feel they are precluded from engaging with them.*

Concerns and Potential Problems

One clear conclusion can be drawn from all the surveys; namely people anticipate more problems than are ever experienced in reality. This is most clearly seen in the survey of employers in Borders Region, around half of whom had no experience of having a person with learning disabilities on their workforce but the other half did have such an experience. Both groups were asked to rate the risks associated with employing such a worker. One group had to do this based on what they think might be required whereas the other employers could answer from their experience. As the figures overleaf illustrate, the results were markedly different.

Likewise shop-keepers with no experience of serving customers who had a learning disability were more likely to anticipate problems than were actually reported by those who had had this experience - 20% compared to 5%.

Percentage of Employers Reporting Problems

Employers... *Possible risks*	*no experience*	*experience*
Safety problems	81%	42%
Longer to learn	62%	25%
Less competent at job	62%	17%
Slower to do job	62%	17%
Inflexible	44%	0%

Similar results have been obtained in surveys of neighbours living adjacent to existing group homes and those living in areas with no residences. These were the anticipated and reported problems found in the Central Region survey.

Percentage of Neighbours Reporting Problems

Neighbours... *Possible problems*	*no experience*	*experience*
Property values drop	28%	7%
Insufficient supervision	24%	12%
Violent and irresponsible	19%	6%
Danger to children	16%	4%
Noisy, create disturbance	16%	8%

Overall three quarters of the people who had experienced living adjacent to group homes report no problems arising whereas only one third of the people living in areas with no existing group home were confident that no problems would arise. Once again, many problems are more imagined than real.

One problem though did keep recurring. Two-thirds of the neighbours surveyed in Central Region felt embarrassed at meeting people with learning disabilities and did not know how to react to them. Likewise shop keepers in Dundee identified two specific concerns they had; how to cope with indistinct or difficult speech and knowing what to do if someone had an epileptic fit.

However in all surveys many respondents were also able to see potential benefits for themselves as well as for people with learning disabilities either working or living in the community. Among the benefits rated highest by employers were: 'honesty; job satisfaction for worker; unlikely to cause trouble; hard-working and friendliness'.

Likewise residents of housing estates mentioned 'changes in attitudes and behaviours thereby providing a good community in which children grow up; positive feelings through opportunities to help others; provides employment for local people'.

Implications

● *Checking with local people regarding their direct experiences puts into perspective the concerns and problems anticipated by people who have had no contact. Indeed such people are likely to prove better advocates than professional workers or family carers who could be thought to have a vested interest.*

● *Knowing the specific concerns of local people makes it easier to devise educational inputs suited to their needs. These concerns vary with different community groups.*

● *Community educators should beware of becoming too focused on the problems. The promotion of possible benefits is often neglected.*

● *A central concern for many is the anticipated embarrassment of not knowing what to say or being unable to cope with unusual behaviours. Bland reassurances to 'act normally' or 'be yourself' are unlikely to be effective. Rather the active support and example of a third person is required for the initial meetings.*

Supporting People in the Community

Community care means more than merely living in the community. In some form or other, it presumes care by the community. But how willing are people to be involved in caring?

Several surveys began by asking whether or not the policy of people with learning disabilities living in their local communities was on the whole a good idea ... a not so good idea ... or they had no opinion.

Support for community care was highest in Dundee and Borders Region (84% rating it a good idea) but lower in Glasgow (77%) and lower still in Central Region (63%). The latter figure masked a wide variation across different areas. Under half of the people (48%) living close to the mental handicap hostel deemed community care a good idea whereas three-quarters of those living near a group home felt it to be so.

Some of the variation in people's opinions derive from their age, their past experiences and their beliefs. For example, people under 40 are more disposed to care in the community; people who had regular contact with this group favoured community care; but people who anticipate problems arising in their neighbourhoods are less likely to favour community care.

The reasons given for supporting care in the community centred around two basic beliefs. First, that 'these people deserve the same chance as others' and second, that 'they are able to integrate into community life'. Other respondents mentioned specific benefits it would bring to people with disabilities, such as increased contacts with family and friends, and to become more independent. This is how two Dundee respondents put it:

> *It lets these people lead as normal a life as possible within the local area, that is to shop, mix with folk in pubs, travel on public transport, in short to be accepted as themselves.*

> *It is about time they are treated as humans and not as something different. They would learn more in the community and we would understand them.*

By contrast reservations about care in the community centred around a concern that people would not get the support and help which they needed or that they would be at risk of abuse or exploitation. Another Dundonian had strong views:

> *There is no longer a caring system in our NHS and some patients are forced to look after themselves without proper care and attention from trained staff. It is all too often left to family, friends and neighbours who do not have, and never will have the experience to handle those unfortunate persons. If we broke an arm, we would not expect our neighbours to mend it and look after us.*

Other misgiving were more selfish - 'uses up houses; these people are a danger to others'.

Willingness to be personally involved

All the surveys in different ways, explored people's willingness to become personally involved. However, the problem with this approach is that their expressions of interest may not translate into reality. Hence it is changes in the *patterns* of response rather than the actual percentages of people expressing interest which are likely to be most reliable.

Around two-thirds of people in Glasgow housing schemes expressed a willingness to attend a coffee evening locally; half were willing for people with disabilities to visit their home but fewer than a quarter were willing to participate in a befriending scheme. However when opportunities for work experience placements were explored with shop-keepers and employers in Borders Region and Dundee, only one in twenty expressed any degree of willingness.

The message is clear, only a small minority of people are willing to make a committed response but given the data documented earlier about lack of contact and perceived problems this is hardly surprising. Our attention needs to be focused on the wider group who do express a willing for some form of personal contact. What is it that distinguishes these people from others who are unwilling for any form of contact?

Statistical analyses of data from the two largest surveys (involving nearly 760 people in total) provides some leads. The people expressing a willingness for involvement were more likely:

- to have had contact in the past with people who have a learning disability;
- to have moved into the area within the last five years;
- to know more of their neighbours by name;
- to live in local authority or rented housing.

Implications

♦ *Support for community care policies varies both within as well as between regions with sizeable numbers of people expressing reservations. Failure to address these concerns could ultimately jeopardise funding for new styles of services. In particular reassurances need to be given about funding for services and support staff.*

♦ *Promoting people's rights for equal opportunities while emphasising their competency to live in the community are themes which many people in the community would echo.*

♦ *An indeterminate number of people exist within communities who would be willing for some involvement if asked. Local surveys can identify possible allies and sources of help.*

◆ *Personal contacts with people who have a learning disability rather than putting people off, appears to win them over. Hence the priority to create even more opportunities for people to meet.*

◆ *Certain neighbourhoods are more welcoming than others to groups of people with a learning disability. Taking time to determine the characteristics of neighbourhoods through community consultations would help services seek out those districts where the risks of active opposition are lower and the chances for social integration are higher.*

Further Reading

Gallup Polls (1981). Our image of the disabled and how ready we are to help, *New Society,* January 1st.

McConkey, R. (1987). *Who Care? Community Involvement with Handicapped People,* London, Souvenir Press.

McConkey, R. (1990). Community reactions to group Homes: Contrasts between people living in areas with, and without a Group Home, In W.I.Fraser (ed.), *Key Issues in Mental Retardation Research,* London, Routledge.

Market and Opinion Research International (1982). *Public attitudes towards the mentally handicapped: Research Study conducted for MENCAP,* London, Mencap.

CHANGING ATTITUDES - WHAT WORKS?

In later sections of the book, we shall spell out in detail specific approaches for educating communities. This section contains a summary of the key elements which experience internationally has shown to be effective and for which there is some documented evidence of success; although often this is quite sparse.

Planned Personal Contacts

One consensus emerges from all the international research which has been done on changing attitudes towards people with disabilities, namely that enjoyable interactions with a peer who is handicapped invariably produces positive changes. Researchers note too that it is the *quality* of the contact rather than quantity, which is important and they do warn that certain contacts may actually increase than decrease the public's negative impressions.

Successful contacts are more likely if:

■ People meet in ordinary places rather than in specialist centres. Hence in a short programme on mental handicap used in Irish secondary schools, a group of trainees from the local centre came to visit the pupils in their school rather than the more usual arrangement of pupils visiting special centres.

■ People share an activity together rather than relying solely on conversation.   Business executives who shared a two-day 'wilderness' expedition with people who had physical disabilities were more willing to consider employing such a person in their firms.

■ First contacts are with people with whom they can communicate relatively easily.   As their confidence increases they can be introduced to people with more severe handicaps.

■ The presence of a 'mediator', someone who knows the person with disabilities can help smooth introductions; identify topics of mutual interest, set up activities, overcome communication difficulties and more generally act as a role model for the person who is not used to interacting with people who have disabilities.

■ People have more opportunities to interact in small groups. Pairing unfamiliar people with one or two individuals who have a disability is preferable to meeting in large groups.

■ The people meeting are about the same age, from the same area and ethnic background and so on.   The attitudes of teachers in mainstream schools was more affected by meeting peers with disabilities than children from special schools.

More *negative experiences* are likely to result from:

☐ The public being taken on a tour of specialist facilities with little or no opportunity to meet people with a disability.

☐ The person with disabilities displaying unusual or aggressive behaviours; or behaving in an antisocial manner during the meeting.

☐ Meetings which occur unexpectantly and for which people are unprepared can produce embarrassment and avoidance.

☐ People having to cope with meeting large groups of people with disabilities at the same time; say four or more people with learning disabilities who may all vie for the newcomer's attention.

Sad to say, these negative experiences are still commonplace in specialist services and often form the first introductions for students on placements; local officials and politicians on 'fact-finding' visits; family members and even other people with disabilities who are joining the service.

Interesting and relevant information

Although negative attitudes may stem from inaccurate information; the corollary of creating more positive attitudes by giving information holds true only under a number of conditions.

● The information needs to emphasise the personal attributes of people with disabilities rather than features of the impairment. For example, "Andrew is a Rangers Supporter with Down's syndrome. His extra chromosome doesn't stop him from cheering on his team."

● An emphasis needs to be placed on people's abilities in order to counter the public's stereotype of dis-ability being *in*-ability. Abilities can include a sense of humour; memory for names; love of the seaside and so on.

● The information needs to be relevant for the target group and addresses their particular concerns. Information targeted at primary school youngsters needs to be different from that provided for potential employers.

● People with a disability, or parents of a child with a disability, are among the best providers of information as they can speak from their personal experience and in ways to which an audience can relate. Likewise people from the community who have experienced a change of attitude themselves can be used to share their experiences with others; for instance, neighbours living beside a group home.

● Information must be easily understood. Short sentences using simple words and plenty of examples will communicate your message more effectively than textbook prose.

That said, there is very little evidence that information per se, changes attitudes. Equally, if not more important, is the way information is presented; a theme we take up in the next section.

Once again, information can *perpetuate* negative images of disability. Particular criticism has been levelled at the fund-raising information produced by national charities. Unwittingly their appeal for the public's sympathy has led them to promote unflattering portrayals of people with disabilities. The most infamous of which was Mencap's poster campaign showing a sorrowful child with Down's Syndrome and the caption; 'Some families have a cross to bear this Christmas'.

Likewise, national television programmes which feature the 'plight' of disabled people may distance the viewer from ever helping by increasing the feeling that "they couldn't cope" and "aren't the parents or staff marvellous who do that sort of work".

Finally, there is little evidence to support the widely held-belief that national advertising campaigns on television, radio or billboards, make the public any better informed or disposed to helping. Indeed the people most likely to attend to such messages are those already involved and interested, such as family members or staff. Precisely the same phenomena is found with car advertisements. People read more avidly the adverts for the cars they have just purchased! In both instances, the advertising helps to confirm our choices and beliefs and while this might be laudable and necessary we cannot justify the expense of advertising campaigns on the grounds that it will change the minds of others who think differently.

Multi-media presentations

The advice here is simple: do not rely on one method to get your message across. Videos, talks, leaflets, posters, cartoons and discussions can all be used to good effect.

♦ Video has the advantage of portraying people with disabilities in a range of ordinary settings while also providing implicit role models for viewers as to how they might interact with them. Locally produced videos have added appeal.

♦ Leaflets and posters must contain illustrations. Colour photographs are preferable to black-white. The advent of colour photocopying has helped reduce the costs.

♦ Puppet shows and drama productions have also been used to convey serious messages about discrimination and disability in a fun and appealing way.

♦ Use can be made of 'activity learning' techniques such as having to use signs to communicate or shopping around the town in a wheelchair. Although used more frequently with children and young people; they are applicable to all ages.

♦ Mock 'debates' in which people are allocated roles have also produced changes in expressed attitudes, e.g. swimmers complaining to management about the number of people with disabilities using the pool.   Time must be allowed for guided discussion of the issues raised otherwise the learning value of the activity can be lost.

Changing Behaviours

As any health educator will tell you, the most difficult part of the job is changing people's behaviour. Likewise with disability, we can increase people's knowledge and apparently change their attitudes for the better but they still behave no differently when confronted with a person who has a disability; remaining apathetic or even antagonistic.

Are our educational efforts then a waste of time?   Are they no more than efforts in self-justification undertaken by professionals in collusion with people who are disabled?   Perhaps they are or they could become so. The acid test though is simple. Are people with disabilities more involved in communities and are they meeting more people?

Some would argue, with justification, that these outcomes can be achieved without resorting to specific 'educational' campaigns. Rather our energies should be directed to ensuring that from a young age, children and adults with disabilities are part of community life. In this way, the general public are 'forced' to change their behaviours.

○ Babies and toddlers with disability attend local groups with their mothers;

○ Pre-schoolers are enrolled in neighbourhood playgroups and nurseries

○ Children with a marked disability may attend the same primary school as their brothers and sisters;

○ Youngsters join youth organisations and sports clubs

○ Young adults attend Colleges of Further Education and find places on work experience schemes.

○ People with disabilities are employed in local businesses

○ Men and women live in ordinary housing, either on their own, with their partners or in small groups.

Indeed, the evidence is now indisputable that creating contacts of this sort does indeed make the public - employers, neighbours, teachers - change their behaviour and attitudes. Hence such initiatives must be to the fore in our services. Equally they force us to redefine what we mean by educating communities.

Of course all of the endeavours listed above are deeply 'educational' for the participants concerned although the people instigating them, for instance parents of a toddler with Down's syndrome, may not label them as an initiative in community education. For them the driving force is the well-being of their child.

However more systematic initiatives may still be needed; most usually when some form of resistance or objection are anticipated or experienced from community groups. Past instances include neighbours of certain housing estates and teachers in primary schools. Here the experiences of others in similar circumstances can be especially useful in devising local educational initiatives. The effort expended on them can be justified on long term dividends and not just in short-term benefits.

Contact with people who have a disability may result in people from the community wanting to know more. Educational initiatives in response to public 'demand' can take many forms but once again, the better planned and presented they are, the more likely they are to increase the public's interest and involvement.

Similarly, people already in contact with people who have disabilities may need further education, even though they do not request it. Hence the educational inputs given to staff in services so that a better quality of service is given. Neighbours, co-workers and fellow-students could equally benefit from 'in-service training'.

Finally, educational inputs can prepare the way for community placements, for example, when resettling sizeable numbers of people from a mental handicap hospital. The intention here would be to replace gossip and hearsay with accurate information and to illustrate what this might mean for local people. Such initiatives are especially necessary with certain groups such as local politicians, for whom no amount of contact with the hospital patients would provide the answers they want.

In sum, educating the community about disability is a multi-facet task. Certain approaches and methods have proved to be successful but these need to be incorporated into a coherent strategy if the ultimate goal of involving people with disabilities in their local communities is to be attained.

Selected References

Acton, H. & Zarbatany, L. (1988). Interaction and performance within co-operative groups: Effects on non-handicapped students' attitudes toward their mildly mentally retarded peers, *American Journal on Mental Retardation,* 93, 16-23.

Donaldson, J. (1980). Changing attitudes toward handicapped persons: a review and analysis of research, *Exceptional Children,* 35, 5-22.

Hogan, R. (1986). Gaining community support for group homes, *Community Mental Health Journal,* 22, 117-126.

Harrison, B. & Tomes, A. (1990). Employers' attitudes to the employment of people with mental handicaps: An empirical study, *Mental Handicap Research,* 3, 196-213.

LeUnes, A. (1975). Institutional tour effects on attitudes relating to mental retardation, *American Journal of Mental Deficiency,* 79, 732-735.

Levy, J.M. et al (1991). Employment of persons with severe disabilities in large businesses in the United States, *International Journal of Rehabilitation Research,* 14, 323-332.

Leyser, Y. et al. (1986). Direct intervention to modify attitudes toward the handicapped by community volunteers: The Learning about Handicaps Programme, *Educational Review,* 38, 229-236.

McCleary, I.D. & Chesteen, S.A. (1990). Changing attitudes of disabled persons through outdoor adventure programmes, *International Journal of Rehabilitation Research,* 13, 321-324.

McConkey, R. and McCormack, B. (1983). *Breaking Barriers: Educating people about disability,* London, Souvenir Press.

McConkey, R. et al (1984). Preparing young people to meet mentally handicapped adults: A controlled study, *American Journal of Mental Deficiency,* 88, 691-694.

McConkey, R. et al (1993). Neighbours' reaction to community services: Contrasts before and after services open in their locality, *Mental Handicap Research,* 2, 131-141.

Rees, L.M. et al (1991).   Do attitudes toward persons with handicap really shift over time?   Comparison between 1975 and 1988, *Mental Retardation,* 29, 81-86.

Russel, T. & Ayer, F.E. (1988). The effect of a direct-mail informational campaign on attitudes of industrial managers toward the mentally retarded population, *Journal of Mental Deficiency Research,* 32, 183-193.

Shearer, A. (1984). *Think Positive: Advice on presenting people with a mental handicap,* Brussels, ILSMH.

Sturmey, P. (1993). The readability and human interest of information leaflets from major British charities: An unintelligible and boring replication?, *Mental Handicap Research,* 6, 174-183.

Townsend, M.A.R. et al (1993). Children's attitudes toward peers with intellectual disability, *Journal of Intellectual Disability Research,* 37, 405-411.

THE VIEWS OF PEOPLE WITH LEARNING DISABILITIES

People who have been labelled as having learning disabilities have much to gain from a community which is informed about their needs. Equally they are the people who suffer most from an ignorant and hurtful public. A number of workshops were organised under the aegis of the Educating Communities Network aimed at hearing the views and experiences of people with learning disabilities. People came from different parts of Scotland, accompanied by staff from a day centre or residence. More service-users attended than did service providers and we had a chance to hear from invited speakers how people with disabilities have been involved in educating their local communities.

The aims of the workshops

We tried to find answers to four questions:

- WHY bother educating the community?
- WHO needs educating?
- WHAT do they need to know
- HOW might we tell them?

Our speakers were:

✿ Stella Morris, Values into Action (Scotland)

✿ Kate Munro, volunteer trainer with S.E.A.T.I.D., Glasgow.
   (A group of people with physical disabilities who provide Disability Awareness training)

✿ Majorie Arthurs and Yvonne McLaren, from Barnardo's Advocacy Service, Edinburgh.

✿ Craig Mullay, Pamela Robbie and Muriel Rice,
   Kemback Resource Centre, Dundee.

Much of the day was spent in six working groups which gave
participants an opportunity to share their experiences and produce
recommendations for action.

Why Bother?

People with a disability have had bad experiences.   Educating
people about our disability should stop that from happening.
Experiences such as:

> * Name calling from children
> * Teenagers who try to take money off you
> * People staring at you
> * Trouble from GPs
> * Trouble from churches
> * Parents/ carers treating us like children
> * Bad neighbours - always complaining
> * People who mean well but getting it all wrong -
>   'patronisers'.
> * Staying at home because nobody to go out with
> * Youngsters knocking your door and running
>   away
> * People don't take time to listen

New possibilities can open up for us if we educate people about
our disability.

> ☐ Employment
> ☐ Access to courses at college
> ☐ Night classes
> ☐ Raise awareness of professional people
> ☐ Get to know more people

☐ Get an active welcome from pubs, bus companies
☐ Get out and about more
☐ Go to football matches

In sum:

> *"The world's a better place when people
> with disabilities are in it"*

Who Needs Educating?

> *"Everyone who has had no involvement
> with the disability"*
> BUT
> *"Pick a bunch of people and work
> out what to say to them"*

Among the people who got a special mention were:

☐ Influential people - MPs and Councillors
☐ School kids .... Pre-schoolers .... Students ....
Teachers
☐ DSS people
☐ Police
☐ Social Workers Community Workers
☐ Doctors ... nurses .... medical people
☐ Bus companies
☐ Licensed Victuallers Association
☐ Shop owners - access problems
☐ Local residents and communities

☐ Planners and architects
☐ Potential employers
☐ People in media - newspapers; children's TV
  presenters
☐ Staff in services who don't listen to you

Don't forget parents and carers; and people with learning disabilities!

Because ...

☐ They need to know their rights
☐ How to deal with our hang-ups
☐ Fear of offending other people
☐ Not knowing how to treat people
☐ Parents keep us under too much supervision

What Do We Want To Say?

"Disability is an equal opportunities issue; not a medical issue."

"People with disabilities have few choices and few rights in our society"

HOW CAN WE GET THE MESSAGE ACROSS?

"Changing attitudes is very hard work"
"People are not interested in worthy talks
about the disabled. Work on what they want
to know"

People at the workshop told us about what they had tried or their ideas for what might work.

☼ Help other people; get involved in voluntary work -
   demonstrate our skills

☼ Do a charity walk for Children in Need

☼ Take part in sponsored swim or sponsored keep-fit

☼ Be good neighbours - invite them to party

☼ Carrying out a neighbourhood survey to find out
   local perceptions of the day centre

☼ Have a cheese and wine party in the centre

☼ Gala days with stalls, bands, pony rides

☼ Share our centre with other groups - they can use it for
   bowling; old time dancing etc.

☼ Join in with other people to learn new things

☼ Educate our families - have a family group; they could take
   an Open University course

✪ Hold an art exhibition

✪ Put on plays, drama and concerts with other groups

✪ Make a video of the town showing access problems. Show it to local councillors

✪ Have a display of photographs in the local library to show what people with disabilities can do

✪ Local radio and TV - good reports - positive images NOT patronising

✪ Photographs in local media such as free newspapers!

✪ Special Olympics - winning medals

✪ Go to talk to small groups in pre-schools, primary and secondary schools, youth clubs and such like

✪ Encourage volunteers to come and help us

✪ Meet local politicians and officials to tell them what we need

✪ Take part in local events - display stand at shows; work demonstrations

Among the other thoughts which people had:

● We need to start right from birth

● People with disabilities need to be seen in television programmes - soaps; children's TV.

● Present information in a positive, upbeat way

- Bomb special things - schools first!

- Use people with learning disabilities to teach other people, such as hospitals doctors and nurses

- Encourage advocacy. Barnardo's recruit people from the community to act as an advocate for others. These people have friends. Through them others get to know more about disability.

In sum:

- Be a good listener
- Be positive in ourselves
- Challenge people
- Be confident
- Enjoy life

WHERE NEXT?

Ideas for what could happen next:

- ☐ Form a campaigning organisation to change views, names used
- ☐ Gain a voice within your own service organisation; set up a member's council; User's group or worker's committee
- ☐ Network with other groups
- ☐ Promote activities for other people within your centre
- ☐ Have a conference organised and run by adults with learning difficulties
- ☐ Have a newsletter
- ☐ Go to small groups of people - school children and youth clubs
- ☐ Get trained to work on educating people about disability

☐ Find out what happens in other countries
☐ People with different disabilities could work together
   as they have a common experience of discrimination.

Conclusions

People with and without disabilities need to
WORK TOGETHER!

* If left to people with disabilities, it's an uphill struggle for them; they have no contacts; they may lack confidence.

* If left to people without disabilities; they lack insights into what it means to be disabled.

Together we can create positive images and positive action

FURTHER INFORMATION

Contact Addresses

Values Into Action, Oxford House, Derbyshire Street, London E2 6HG

People First, Oxford House, Derbyshire Street, London E2 6HG (Self-advocacy Network)

Skill: National Bureau for students with Disabilities, 336 Brixton Road, London, SW9 7AA

S.E.A.T.I.D. (Strathclyde Education and Training In Disability) Fernan Street Complex, Fernan Street, Glasgow G32 7HF

Barnardo's Advocacy Service, 235 Corstorphine Road, Edinburgh EH12 7AR

Kemback Resource Centre, Kemback Street, Dundee DD4 6PG

Useful Books

Video First: Ideas for using video for self-advocacy.

Sticking Up for Yourself: Self-advocacy and people with learning difficulties, by K. Simons and J. Carter.

Both booklets available from: Norah Fry Research Centre, 32, Tyndall's Park Road, Bristol, BS8 1PY

Workshop Participants

Bonnington Resource Centre, Edinburgh - Deborah Waugh,
    Pauline Crombie, June Gillis, Heather Fyffe
Inverurie, Abderdeenshire - Hettie Thomson, Linda Wylie, Morag Keith
Barrhead Project, Glasgow - Margaret Gruber, Jessie Hannigan,
    Elaine Thomson, Monica Carr
Elcap, East Lothian - Philip Russell, Sylvia Archibald
Bingham House, Edinburgh - Sarah Jane Davies, Bruce Roberts,
    Keith Donald
Garbhenn, Fort William - Liz Reid, Ron Grattan, Sandy Angus
Grindlay Court, Edinburgh - Amanda Carnie, Katherine Haddaw
Gogarburn Hospital, Edinburgh - Penny McDade, Robert Bell
Peebles - Mary Bishop
People First Borders - James Dallas
Reiver Enterprises, Galashiels - Gavin Curran
Cherry Road Centre, Bonnyrigg - Jane Fairnie, Alan Watson

A STRATEGY FOR
EDUCATING COMMUNITIES

Looking back over the past twenty years or so to when educating communities about disability first started to emerge as a specific endeavour, a number of fundamental shifts can be detected in which the task is now conceived. These are:

✿ *A focus on the person not the disability*
Priority is given to creating enjoyable, face-to-face meetings rather than providing formal talks or literature.

✿ *Educating communities is a process rather than an event*
Sustained changes in the public's attitudes and behaviour do not come about from a single event. Rather they result from a range of initiatives from a diversity of sources so that members of the public accumulate experiences and knowledge.

✿ *The goal is to build inclusive communities rather than give information*
Educating the community is not an end in itself, nor should it get distorted into a charity appeal. Rather it is the essential complement to all the careful planning which goes into preparing young people with a learning disability for living in the community. Such programmes may develop their talents but equally necessary are the creation of openings and opportunities within communities which they cannot produce by themselves.

Many factors have brought about these changes; the advocacy of people with disabilities and their families; the change in service systems from institution to community based and the results of early efforts in this field; all of which have been elaborated in earlier sections.

However old thinking still lingers on. In an attempt to give it the kiss of death, this section describes a strategy for educating communities which embraces all the 'stake-holders' - people with learning disabilities; family carers; professional workers; service providers and politicians - and makes the task everyone's responsibility while recognising that the various players can contribute in different ways according to their opportunities and talents. The result is a multi-facet task which never ends as people's needs change and new members join communities.

Essential Elements

The essential elements of the strategy are these:

◆   The needs and aspirations of local people with learning disabilities determine the agenda for educating communities.

◆   The priority is to create opportunities for enjoyable interactions between people with disabilities and their peers in a range of community settings.

◆   Information about disability is conveyed in a way that promotes positive images of people with disability; corrects misconceptions and addresses the concerns of communities.

◆   An analysis needs to be made locally of the various 'communities' which can contribute significantly to the lives of people with disabilities and educational initiatives are targeted specifically at them.

◆   The task can be undertaken by various groups of people but their efforts may require support and should prove more effective when co-ordinated around common goals.

♦   The success of such initiatives is reflected in the increased participation of people with learning disabilities in community activities

The rationale for the first three elements have been covered in previous sections.   Here we concentrate on the idea of target communities; we identify the range of people already involved in educating communities and tackle the thorny issue as to how this strategy can be put into practice.

A Community of Communities

The old notion of geographical communities - people living and working within a common locality - is fast breaking down in modern society and in cities especially.   Replacing it are communities made up of people with common interests drawn from quite wide areas. Defined this way, the public are members of many different communities albeit with varying degrees of allegiances.   Hence a 30 year old women could belong to various communities - badminton club, playgroup committee member, labour party supporter, the police, residents association and a shopper at Safeway!

Conceiving of communities in this way makes it easier to identify those sections of the community who are a priority target in any educational programme.   For example you may chose to focus your energies at certain influential groups, who by the nature of their work come into contact with people who have learning disabilities, for example leisure centre attendants, local bus drivers/conductors, police constables and officials in housing departments.   All of whom could make life easier for these people if they had a better understanding of the disability.

Or attention might be focused on groups who in turn could become educators of others, such as newspaper reporters or local radio presenters, senior pupils in secondary schools, apprentices and students in training.

More specifically, the common needs of people with learning disabilities will identify priority groups. For example if several people wish to work in cafes or restaurants, the owners of such businesses might be targeted for special attention.

A focus on 'target groups' also makes the task more manageable in that the different but particular needs of each group are more easily identified and addressed. What local councillors want or need to know about learning disability can be quite different to the concerns of workers in playgroups about to enrol a child with Down's Syndrome.

Last but most significantly, the emphasis on specific groups can make the task less daunting, especially if the educators involved in the endeavour already are members of the targeted groups or know someone who already is. Such 'circles of friends' as they have become known are potent ways of introducing people with disabilities into communities.

From our experiences with the Network, the most popular 'target' groups singled out for educational initiatives in Scotland are: schools; employers; neighbours of community residents; the media; politicians and churches. Hence in Section 2 of the book, we focus specifically on what has been, or could be done, to address the particular needs and concerns of these communities. Similar approaches could be adopted with other communities.

Community Educators

The image of the 'expert' lecturer lingers on, unintentionally perpetuated perhaps by the many professionals who earn a livelihood in our disability services and who are invited to talk about their work to community groups. In reality, this sort of contribution appears to have little impact except to boost the morale of the lecturer, and their time and talents could be better deployed in other ways.

More importantly though, the education of communities does not need to be done formally, nor even identified as such. Much effective work is already being carried out by a range of people as they go about their usual routines. Rather they need to be actively involved in more systematic efforts. I am thinking of:

● **People with learning disabilities:** They are often their own best advocates if given the chance. Their involvement in the enterprise should break down the 'them' and 'us' mentality that so pervades current thinking.

● **Parents and relatives:** They have the emotional involvement and the direct experience which can silence the sceptic. As most are already connected into local communities through family and friends, they can help gain access to many community groups.

● **Sympathetic people from the community:** This includes 'volunteer helpers', employers who have taken people on work experience and next door neighbours to community homes. They are creditable witnesses to others in the community; people with whom they can easily identify. Through their contacts, they too are able to link into other groups.

● **Front-line service staff:** Their role may already involve contacts with the community through neighbours, shopkeepers and health centre staff, and much can be gained from their experiences. They are aware too of the particular needs among people with disability. Other professional workers may have a special expertise they can share with others, e.g. how best to communicate with certain people; what to do if a person has an epileptic seizure.

● **Status figures in the community:** Such as doctors, councillors, clergy. Their advice and ability to open doors into communities may prove valuable even though they may be the first to admit that they know nothing about learning disabilities. But it's what they know about the local community that makes their contribution valuable when planning local initiatives.

Whose job is it to educate communities?

The above listing reminds us of the possibilities as to who can be engaged in educating communities but nothing will be done if each is leaving it up to the others. And how can the efforts of these groups be brought together in a common endeavour? In sum, who's taking the lead in educating communities?

Our experiences with the Educating Communities Network suggests that professional workers are to the fore. Of the 60 or so active members all but a handful are employees of Regional Council Social Work or Education Departments (48%) ; Voluntary sector services (32%) or Health Boards (17%) and they are working in a range of services; including day services and employment schemes; residential services; leisure and befriending schemes and community education.

However when asked to identify the most common obstacles they had encountered in attempting to educate local communities, the two most commonly mentioned were; 'too much other work' (66%) and 'no organisational policy or agreement on what to do' (34%).

The Network members were however under no delusions about their own importance to the process. Rather they considered the people best placed to undertake the job of educating communities, to be:

- ☐ people with learning disabilities (with support)
- ☐ teachers in primary and secondary schools
- ☐ families of people with learning disabilities.

Generally they rated themselves in fourth place!

Similarly, they assigned *responsibility* for ensuring that education of communities takes place to:

- ☐ Central Government
- ☐ Social Work Departments
- ☐ Community Education

Very few rated it the responsibility of service providers.

What then should be the role of professional, i.e. paid staff in disability services if they disclaim responsibility for the task and feel that others are better at undertaking it?

For me the answer is simple, they are the instigators of action and mobiliser of resources. They know well the particular needs and aspirations of the people with disabilities; they are employed to meet these needs and through their employing agencies they have access to contacts with other people and resources. None of the other possible educators are so well placed.

But for front-line staff to undertake this new role effectively, organisational support is essential.

First, the funding agencies - Central Government and Social Work Departments especially - must make a clear commitment to the education of local communities and allocate resources for this endeavour. Community care plans, for example, could specify local targets and set out strategies for how these could be attained.

Second, service providers in both the statutory and independent sectors should include commitments to community involvement and their operations should reflect this. Certain posts might be designated to further these objectives or the job descriptions of workers widened to provide for greater involvement with local communities. Needless to add, managerial support and guidance in such endeavours is vital in order to establish and sustain new work practices, as are opportunities for in-service training.

Making a serious commitment to educating communities requires changes to the policies and practices at all levels within our existing service systems. The fact that this is still the case is symptomatic of the changes still required for them to truly become community, rather than disability focused.

Partnerships

The emphasis on services as instigators of community education is not to suggest that this is done solely by service personnel. On the contrary, the expectation is that they will work in partnership with others, especially people with learning disabilities; their family carers and local 'allies' from the community. Indeed their efforts might be directed at facilitating and supporting such groups to undertake their own initiatives and joining with them in lobbying for the necessary resources.

In time too, other groups could take over the responsibility, especially as they gain expertise and confidence in the task. I am thinking particularly of self-advocacy groups of people with learning disability. Although some may be well equipped to do this already, our experiences in Scotland suggest that this is not generally so. However, people with physical and sensorial disabilities are increasingly to the fore in promoting greater community awareness.

Ultimately the hope would be that communities themselves take the initiative in consulting and adapting to the needs of people with disabilities. This would recognise their status as full and equal members of that community. But without being unduly pessimistic, that day seems far off.

Evaluation of community initiatives

The strategy promoted here emphasises the importance of local initiatives. This means that it is unlikely that people from outside the district will undertake this work although regional or national initiatives could supply useful support. Such an approach has many advantages but it can also be wasteful in the sense that local groups through naivety may make the same mistakes as others have done elsewhere. Too often decisions are made on false presumptions.

I end then with a plea for local groups to document their experiences in a way which can be shared with others. This can be done most simply through team reviews; when all members of the team share their perceptions as to what worked and what they feel needs changing.

More ambitiously, reactions can be collected systematically from the targeted group by means of questionnaires or interviews. Enquiries can be made as to what they got out of your educational endeavours and their suggestions for changes. Particularly useful would be their perceptions before and after the programme started.

In later sections we describe some of the techniques which local teams can use to consult with communities and to evaluate the impact of their initiatives. There is a real dearth of published material on changing community perceptions from which others can learn.

Unresolved Issues

Thus far, our attention has been exclusively focused on people with learning disabilities. But on many issues they have much in common with other disability groups yet there is a great reluctance to join forces; often on the premise that 'we are not like them'. People with physical disabilities do not want to be associated with people who have learning disabilities while they in turn are keen to emphasis that they are not mentally ill. The real danger is that one disability group devalues another in their keenness to project themselves. We still have much to learn about working together towards a common community.

Another unresolved issue is the future role of specialist services and their trained workforces. Put simply, there will be less need for both as local communities develop their competence at coping with people who have learning disabilities. Is there a conflict of interest which prevents existing services working wholeheartedly towards the involvement of their service-users in local communities?

Finally, British society has changed radically during the last 30 years and will continue to do so. What if these changes lead to the breakdown of communities as we know them, which could happen if our society becomes more self-centred and competitive; lawlessness and exploitation of the weak increases and family networks become increasingly fractured. Indeed some would argue that already in many city areas, community life barely exists. What then are the prospects for people with learning disabilities under these conditions?

I accept that these three issues would have major ramifications for our present social policy in regard to people with disabilities. However, I am not sufficiently foresightful to anticipate the consequences, suffice to say that being aware of them is at least some safeguard to the complacency which comes from thinking we have got right. Rabbie Burns put it more poetically when he wrote:

> *The best laid plans o'mice an' men;*
> *Gang aft agley* (often go awry)
> *An' lea'e us nought but grief an' pain;*
> *For promis'd joy!*

As you embark on educating communities, I trust you are spared the grief and pain; experiencing instead the promised joy.

Further Reading

McConkey, R. (1991). *Opening Doors: Educating the Community about Mental Handicap,* Glasgow, Enable.

A beginner's guide for anyone who wants to help part of their local community become more aware of the abilities and needs of people with mental handicap.   It offers simple suggestions and examples for identifying target groups and advice about getting the right message across to them. Available from: Enable, 7, Buchanan Street, Glasgow

Schwartz, D.B. (1992). *Crossing the river: Creating a conceptual revolution in community and disability,* Cambridge Mass., Brookline Books.

Presents a new vision as to how services for people with learning disabilities should be conceived and implemented. The central theme is the building of secure relationships among community members, with and without disabilities that are mutually rewarding. Available through booksellers.

Sutcliffe, J. (1990). *Adults with Learning Difficulties: Education for Choice and Empowerment,* Milton Keynes, Open University Press.

Although written to promote continuing education for adults with learning difficulties, the book provides an excellent overview of the new styles of services on offer and how people with this disability can become more integrated into their local community. Plenty of ideas are given for further reading and resources. Available through booksellers.

SECTION 2
TARGET GROUPS

In modern society, geographical communities with a common identity are becoming rarer. Replacing them are communities of people who share a common interest or function. Hence people can belong to many different communities depending on their interests.

In this section, this theme is pursed by focusing on specific community groups who were commonly rated as having a significant role to play in furthering the involvement of people with learning disabilities into their community.

The Educating Communities Network organised a series of one day workshops which explored approaches and methods that had been particularly successful with selected groups. The workshops were led by resource persons who had experience of working with the communities in question. Additional insights and expertise were also provided by the Network members attending. Details of resources and further information appropriate to each community group are given at the end of each section. The six communities examined were:

☐ Working with Schools

☐ Approaching Employers

☐ Reassuring Neighbours

☐ Dealing with the Media

☐ Educating Politicians and Officials

☐ Linking with Churches

Of course, many other 'target groups' could have been included; Health personnel especially GPs, the Police, Shop Assistants and DSS officials were all mentioned frequently. Hopefully, much of the content in this section will enable readers to devise their own strategies for educating these, and yet other communities.

WORKING WITH SCHOOLS

Schools are the target of many community educators. Educating school pupils about learning disabilities has many attractions.

☐ *Captive audience* - school is the one opportunity of giving everyone some information about this disability.

☐ *Opinion forming* - by catching people when they are young, more positive attitudes can be hopefully nurtured.

☐ *Friend-making* - school pupils increasingly could come into contact with youngsters who have learning disabilities, either in schools or through youth activities and sports.

☐ *Name calling and harassment* - people with learning disabilities often report being taunted or harassed by youngsters.

☐ *Volunteer recruitment* - older teenagers could be recruited to help with leisure and recreational activities in their locality.

☐ *Parent education* - as prospective parents, teenagers should hear of how disabilities can be prevented.

☐ *Career choices* - the interest of school-leavers could be kindled to work in services for people with disabilities.

At another level entirely, work with schools can prepare the way for more children with disabilities to be enrolled in their local nursery, primary or secondary school. In this instance, the attitudes and perceptions of teachers are as crucial as those of pupils.

A workshop organised by the Educating Communities Network aimed to share each others' experiences of educating school pupils about people with learning disabilities, review what had 'worked' and what did not,   and, from such discussion, to develop guidelines to help those who wish to pursue this further.   Our guests were:

♢ Patricia Noonan Walsh, Director of Research and Service Developments, St. Michael's House, Dublin.

♢ Paul Dickens, Clinical Psychologist, Royal Scottish National Hospital, Larbert.

They described two innovative school-based projects:

FAST FRIENDS   In Dublin, teenagers with severe mental and physical handicaps are linked with pupils from local secondary schools, through weekly visits.   These are to fit in with the curricula of both St. Michael's House Day Centre and the timetables of the local schools concerned. The planned activities in which the students take part include arts and crafts, physical education and music classes, all within the local secondary schools. Each pupil from St. Michael's House is linked with two pupils from secondary school.

Patricia Walsh emphasised the importance of good planning, and co-operation among staff from all schools concerned.   Sharing of the workload enabled teachers from both St. Michael's House Day Centre and the local secondary schools, to become involved in the planned activities. All the ideas and organisation of activities were initiated by the teachers.

Positive outcomes have been reported by all concerned as a result of this project.   Teachers in the secondary schools report marked increases in confidence, sensitivity and awareness of others in the pupils concerned, which they claim generalises to other areas of their school lives. Parents of the children from St. Michael's

House are greatly encouraged by the new friendships which their children have formed. A video and information pack, with guidelines for those who wish to set up a similar project, is available (details on p. 73)

JUST LIKE US Central Regional Council Education Department in association with the Royal Scottish National Hospital, Lambert have developed a resource package aimed at increasing awareness of learning disabilities, among Primary 6 and 7 children.

The information pack resulted from the joint efforts of a working party, comprising both teachers and professionals from the field of learning disabilities, but developed by teachers. It is designed as a resource for primary school teachers and consists of photographs, a video and information sheets, for teachers to implement as they wish. The emphasis is on flexibility, to enable teachers to convey the information, at their own discretion.

Just Like Us promotes an interactive method of teaching, focusing heavily on discussion and dealing with complex issues, e.g. institutionalisation, in a simple fashion. It also aims to access children's levels of information about and attitudes toward people with learning disabilities, always highlighting the positive side of the individuals' lives, by using case studies.

The project has been implemented in every primary school in Central Region, and plans are already underway to widen its usage. An evaluation of the pilot study indicates that children did retain the information given to them and they had a more positive attitude to those with learning disabilities.

Experiences Of Network Members

Participants in the workshop contributed their experiences of contacts with schools and made recommendations for how this

work could be developed further.   Five key issues were identified
and ideas presented for tackling them.

- Priority messages to get across
- Linking with schools and colleges
- Getting information across
- Forming contacts between students
- Whose job is it ?

Priority Messages

The goal of this work is to increase awareness and induce more
positive attitudes toward people with learning disabilities, and to
encourage beneficial meetings. For this to happen, we need:

◆ To emphasise the individual rights and competencies of those
with learning disabilities.

♦ To highlight the individuality of each member of society, despite their disability or handicap.

♦ To create interest and a willingness among school children, to become involved, without feeling forced to do so.

♦ To educate not only schools, but other groups in society, about the causes of learning disabilities.

♦ Similarly, to differentiate between Mental Illness and Mental Handicap as these are often confused in children's as well as adult's thinking.

(The latter two goals come from survey findings with school children; see p. 76).

Who should education be aimed at? To date, most British and Irish initiatives have been targeted at secondary school students; particularly students from fourth year onwards. The school curriculum in subjects such as Modern Studies provides a useful context for education about disability and this could begin from first year.

Inputs into primary and even nursery schools are also possible although the biggest challenge is explaining 'learning disabilities' in a way which younger children can understand. The growing range of children's books about disability are useful here (see p. 73).

Youth organisations, such as Scouts, and Youth clubs, Playschemes or Sports clubs are also possible targets. Similar strategies can be employed with them as with schools. Community Education workers can be especially helpful in making contacts with such groups.

Strong arguments can be made for giving priority to educating teachers and youth leaders in the first instance, who in turn will go on to work with the young people.   However to date, teacher preparation has usually focused on the needs of children with disabilities in ordinary classrooms.   We shall return to this point later.

Educational inputs could be directed at teachers in training or students on Nursery Nursing and similar courses.

Others have argued for the need for all trainee professional to receive an input on learning disabilities in their training. Particular mention has been made of doctors, nurses and social workers.   Many of the ideas presented in this section would be applicable with these students although the content may be more focused.

Linking with Schools and Colleges

* Selecting a school or college to work with may be very straightforward if, for example, there is only one secondary school in the vicinity. However most people face a choice. Suggestions for coping with this now follow.

* When motivating interest, begin with local contacts who are already known to you, e.g. family or friends who may be, or who may know, teachers. Similar contacts can be made with the leaders of youth groups to assess their level of interest.

* Enquire from local schools if any educational package on disabilities is presently being used.   Or send a letter to local schools, giving information about possible educational packages which they might find helpful.

* Produce an information leaflet outlining your aims and what you have to offer schools. Requesting feedback lets you gauge each school's level of interest.

* Offer to provide an information workshop for teachers.

* Advocate a" bottom-up " approach to change, to ensure maximum ownership of the scheme/project by the teachers, thus allowing professionals from disability services to maintain only a consultative role. For example this can begin with the formation of a working party of highly interested teachers, producing ideas for educative material who seek advice from the "consultants" when necessary.

* Lobby policy makers to ensure that educating school children about learning disabilities, becomes a worthwhile part of the common curriculum.

Getting Information Across

There is no one way to convey such knowledge, however, as mentioned previously, a flexible approach allows for a variety of resources to be employed.

Examples used by the workshop participants have included:

☐ a series of 'talks'
☐ a "one-off" school assembly
☐ a week-end away
☐ summer school, playschemes
☐ a "Fast Friends" type project with regular contacts

Some points to bear in mind:

* The information given should be age appropriate, both in terms of the language and concepts used, as well as in the way it is presented. Simulating being disabled may appeal to nine year olds but leave teenagers cringing with embarrassment.

* A variety of teaching methods and materials should be included in packages as this allows 'teachers' to adapt them to particular classes or lesson contexts.

* Activity learning methods should feature as this enables the learners to better understand the reality of people with learning disabilities. Suggestions include:

> Role Play and Simulations
> Puppet Plays
> Completing Activity Sheets
> Developing Fact Sheets

In all of the above contrasts can be drawn between the experiences of "normal" children and those with learning disabilities.

* Case studies and video clips may help school children to identify both similarities and differences between themselves and young people with learning disabilities, thus exploding any myths they may hold.

* Video programmes can be shown and *discussed*. These can either be ready-made or locally-produced (see Section 4).

* Extracts from feature films, such as "My Left Foot" or "Rain Man", can be used as triggers for discussion.

* Teachers may also wish to use the creative arts as a means of expressing attitudes and changed perceptions. Popular examples

include designing posters, writing poems, composing songs, devising short skits and story-telling.

* Local groups can be invited to give a presentation, such as integrated dance or drama groups. Once again, the educational value of such events is boosted by time for questions and discussion.

* In schools the ideal would be for children to have an input each year about disability so that certain themes can be developed and new ones introduced. Needless to add, this requires careful planning and coordination so that unnecessary repetition and duplication is avoided.

* The reactions of children (and their teachers), to the educational inputs should be obtained systematically to ensure that the aims of the programme are being met and the content adjusted accordingly. Simple questionnaires have been used successfully with children as young as eight years (see p. 75).

Finally, a crucial part of any input must be the opportunity to meet with peers who have a learning disability.

Forming Contacts among Students

One of the easiest ways of ensuring contact is to involve people with disabilities as 'teachers' in the classrooms. Many are able and willing to relate their experiences and on topics such as name-calling have a unique contribution to make. Likewise parents and brothers or sisters of young children with disabilities can be invited to share their experiences and to be questioned by the young people.

Opportunities for personal interactions between students and peers with disabilities takes more effort to organise but it is invariably worthwhile.   Some pointers to bear in mind:

* Acknowledge that not all students will want to be directly involved with the young people with learning disabilities. Allow them to remain at the periphery, if they wish.

* The young people benefit most if they can share an activity together but do give them choices.   Examples include taking visitors on a tour of the school, darts and pool, parachute games, arm-wrestling.   As far as possible the activities chosen should match the competencies and interests of both groups and should encourage interaction among them.   Useful 'contact' sessions can be arranged in the time allotted for a double class period in schools.

* The activity session needs to planned in advance with the young people themselves. This provides opportunities for them to ask 'what if' questions; for instance, "what if I don't understand what they say?"

* Some thought should be given to the setting for the shared activities; a neutral venue may be preferable, e.g. a local leisure centre.

* For the activities, it is often beneficial to link each young person with a learning disability with two school pupils. In this way they can give each other mutual support.

* Young people with learning disabilities should also be prepared in advance for the proposed meeting which should be designed to benefit them as well as the students. This could be done by gradually introducing the idea of meeting with local school pupils, providing sufficient explanation of the aims of the venture and taking any suggestions and wishes into account. Needless to add, those who do not wish to participate are not forced to.

* Although friendships may develop among the groups, they are not, however the prime reason for the meetings. Hence the success of the venture should not be judged by this criterion nor should the creation of friendships be given as a reason for embarking on the venture. This places a much greater onus on everyone concerned. The primary aim remember is to increase able-bodied students' awareness of learning disabilities and to widen the experiences of young people with learning disabilities through visits to local schools and colleges.

Whose Job Is It to Educate Children about Disability?

Three groups are already involved - teachers, professional disability workers and people with disabilities - who sometimes work together, but more often each does their 'own thing'. Here we identify each one's strengths to undertake this task and propose that co-operative working is the ideal.

Teachers Both primary and secondary teachers are well placed to do the job. If they were to do so, then nearly all children would be involved; a continuous programme could be developed over the years of the child's schooling and links could be made more easily with other curriculum subjects. The main drawbacks are most teachers' lack of knowledge of the subject and the pressures from other parts of the curriculum.

Two proposals have been put forward. The job of educating school pupils about disability could become the specialism of one or more teachers, e.g. working alongside Learning Support Teachers.

Secondly, a City and Guilds or ScotVec module on disabilities could be offered through schools and colleges. This would help to ensure a place in the curriculum for at least some pupils.

People with disabilities Their personal experiences add an invaluable dimension to any educational input and reactions from students are often very favourable. However, it places very great demands on individuals if they were to take sole responsibility for this work throughout even one school. Rather they can act as consultants when programmes are being planned and they may be willing to undertake one or two sessions with certain classes.

Disability professionals To date, they have been the chief instigators of programmes within schools, often making the initial approach and taking responsibility for devising and presenting the package. Their obvious advantages are their knowledge and experience of disability coupled with easy access to people with learning disabilities to arrange contact sessions that are beneficial to both groups. Inevitably though, this work is done as an extra to their other responsibilities and while this is tolerable for a 'one-off' project it is difficult to sustain in the longer-term.

The suggestion of having a designated worker within disability services to develop community education initiatives is a favoured solution and one which is operating in a number of services throughout Scotland. Their work is likely to be most effective when they mobilise and support community groups, such as teachers, to undertake the job.

Ideally, a coalition of all three parties would be formed to implement education about disability within schools. In the absence of this, then attempts by any one group are better than nothing and could be a preliminary to joint action.

RESOURCES FOR USE WITH SCHOOLS

Information is arranged in the following sections

- Resource Packs
- Books for Children
- Further Reading
- Survey Findings

Resource Packs
This section contains information about ready-made teaching packages which could be used in schools.

Call Us By Our Names: *A pack about people with special learning needs resulting from mental handicap.*
Kevin Ford and Philip Hope, London, CSV Education, 1991.
Designed for meet the syllabus requirements of the National Curriculum in three areas:

* Personal and Social Education (14-16)
* Pre-vocational Education (14-16)
* Pre-vocational Education (16-18).
Further cross-curriculum links and themes are also noted.

The pack consists of a 72 page work book, based around a series of group activities which are designed to promote thought and discussion about people with learning disabilities. Topics covered include labels, attitudes, human and legal rights, causes and prevention. Photocopiable resource sheets and worksheets are also provided along with a 60 minute video consisting of 16 clips for use during the activities. Further Information from: *CSV Education, 237, Pentonville Road, London N1 9NJ*

Thinking about Mental Handicap: Learning about the lives of people with learning difficulties.
Angie Ash, Penarth, MHNA Publications
Based around eight, three-hour sessions the pack contains Tutor's notes; Information Sheets, Exercise Sheets and Illustrations from which overhead transparencies can be made. The topics include - 'So what is mental handicap'; 'How services have developed over the years' and 'The lives of people with learning disabilities.
Although intended for use on college courses, parts of the pack would be suitable for senior pupils in secondary schools.
Further Information from*MHNA,PO Box 15,Penarth,
South Glamorgan, Wales, CF6 1YP*

Our Lifestyles: An introductory exercise for anyone meeting people with learning difficulties
Hove, Pavilion Training Materials, 1991
Written by a group of people who have learning disabilities this pack consists of a 45 minute exercise aimed at improving people's behaviour when meeting people with disabilities. Topics include being addressed, mealtimes, being at home and happiness. The pack consists of facilitator's notes and 18 exercise cards which can

be photocopied. Further Information from: *Pavilion Training Materials, 42, Lansdowne Place, Hove, East Sussex, BN3 1HH*

Just Like Us
A package aimed at Primary 6 pupils is being field-tested in Central Region, Scotland. Produced by Forth Valley Health Board and Central Region Education Department, the package will consist of teacher's notes, information sheets and a specially made video programme. Further Information from *Director of Nursing Services, Royal Scottish National Hospital,Larbert, FK5 4SD*

Fast Friends: Shared classroom activities for students with and without learning disabilities.
St. Michael's House, Dublin, 1992.
Young people in Dublin have been meeting weekly in secondary schools to share classroom activities such as Physical Education, Arts and Crafts and Music. The information pack contains a short handbook giving guidelines for those wishing to set up similar schemes along with an excellent 23 minute video programme describing the project and giving the reactions of teachers and students. Available from:*St. Michael's House Research, Upper Kilmacud Road, Stillorgan, Co. Dublin, Ireland*

Books for Children
There are a growing number of books featuring characters with a learning disability. The list starts with those suitable for younger children.

I have a mental handicap
Althea, Dinosaur Publications, 1987
Aimed at 5-8 year olds, the series also includes 'I have epilepsy'; 'I can't hear like you' and 'I use a wheelchair'.

Jessy Runs Away & Best Friends,
Rachel Anderson and Shelagh McNicholas, Jets/Young Lions, 1990 & 1991
Both books are aimed at early readers and feature Jessy a girl with Down's syndrome. Good plots and up-to-date illustrations.

I have Down's Syndrome,
Brenda Pettenuzzo, Franklin Watts Publishing, 1987
For older children in primary schools; other titles include - 'I am deaf' and 'I have spina bidifa'.

My Sister is Different
Betty Wright, Blackwell Raintree, 1982
The story of a girl with learning disabilities. Her brother resents having to look after her until the day she gets lost. For older primary children.

Welcome Home Jellybean,
Marlene Shyer, Collins Cascades
The story of a girl with multiple impairments brought home from residential care to live with her parents and brothers. Aimed at teenagers the story is told through the eyes of the brother.

Skallagrig
William Horwood, Penguin, 1988
For older teenagers and young adults. Intertwines stories of life in mental handicap hospitals with the experiences of a multiply handicapped young man; a wizard with computers.

Further Reading

Education about Disability: Curriculum Guidelines.
Scottish Council on Disability, 1989
The booklet provides guidelines for teachers on how to introduce and develop education about disability throughout the curriculum.

The strategies are set out in three main sections - primary, secondary and further education. The increasing demands on the time of teachers and lecturers is recognised and the recommendations in these guidelines are suitably modest. Available from:*Scottish Council on Disability, Princes House, 5, Shandwick Place, Edinburgh EH2 4RG.*

Breaking Barriers: Educating people about mental handicap
Roy McConkey & Bob McCormack, London, Souvenir Press, 1983
Reviews past research on attitudes and the need to educate communities. Seven key elements in formulating community education programmes are examined including meeting disabled people, participant involvement, publicity and the presentation of information. A six-session programme, designed and tested for use in schools with 15-16 year olds, is described along with an extensive listing of resources. Available from booksellers or libraries.

Challenging prejudice through education:
The story of a mental handicap awareness curriculum project,
John Quicke, Karen Beasley & Caroline Morrison, Falmer Press, London, 1990
An inside account of the rationale, development and implementation of awareness project in schools. Available through booksellers.

Meeting Special Needs in Ordinary Schools
Seamus Hegarty, London, Cassells, 1987
An overview of the range of provision opening up for children with disabilities in mainstream education and the factors which contribute to successful integration.

Let's Integrate: Young people with handicaps in youth organisations.
Roger May, Sutton, Printforce, 1987
Documents the experiences of youth leaders of coping with children who have disabilities; useful tips for schools.   Copies available from: *Printforce, 6, Angel Hill Drive,Sutton, Surrey SM1 3BX*

Survey Findings

Kyle, C. and Davies, K. (1991). Attitudes of mainstream pupils towards mental retardation: Pilot study at a Leeds Secondary School, *British Journal of Special Education,* 18, 103-106.

Quicke, J. (1989). Pupil's knowledge of mental handicap: A study of second year pupils in a British Comprehensive school, *International Journal of Rehabilitation Research,* 12, 17-26..

Eggert, D. & Berry, P. (1992). German, Irish and Australian High school students' perceptions of mental handicap, *International Journal of Rehabilitation Research,* 15, 355-360.

Ward, J. et al. (1994). A question of attitudes: Integrating children with disabilities into regular classrooms, *British Journal of Special Education,* 21, 34-39.

An extensive investigation of the attitudes of six groups of educationalists (headteachers; regular teachers; preschool directors etc. - nearly 5,000 people in all) toward the integration in mainstream schools of children with various special educational needs.

APPROACHING EMPLOYERS

An increasingly number of men and women with learning disabilities aspire to having an ordinary job. Yet the common perception of many people in the community is that they cannot work; a feeling sometimes shared by families and some professional workers.

The workshop focused on strategies and techniques which could change these perceptions. Our speakers were -

✿   Christy Lynch, Chief Executive Officer with the K.A.R.E. Association in Ireland and President of the European Association for Supported Employment

✿   Catherine Graham, Community Resource Officer with the Activity and Resource Centre in Dumfries.

✿   Mike Hope, Manager of Auchentibber Resource Centre, High Blantyre.

The content of the guide was further developed in four working groups which gave participants an opportunity to share their experiences and produce recommendations for action. The first part of this booklet focuses on employers while wider issues such as family attitudes and obstacles arising from our service systems are dealt with in the second part.

The topic of paid employment raises other issues, such as implications for the paying of state benefits. The workshop did not attempt to deal with these, most of which are covered in recent publications listed in the resources section at the end. Here our emphasis is on educating employers, co-workers and the wider community about the work potential of people with learning disabilities.

Starting Points

A number of fundamental beliefs underpin the search for productive work for persons with learning disabilities.

● Any person, no matter how severe their disabilities, is capable of productive work *if given the appropriate supports.*

● The attitude of employers is often not the problem. Rather parental concerns, professional scepticism and the benefits bureaucracy pose greater hurdles.

● However, employers often have little previous experience of this disability. Their perceptions of problems is likely to be exaggerated compared to those actually reported by employers with experience. In particular, they think that people require more supervision; more at risk of accidents; slower to learn and less productive.

● Employers with experience of taking people with learning disabilities give as benefits their willingness to work; their dependability and capacity to stick at jobs.

● The attitude of Trade Unions are often positive as they are eager to promote equal opportunities and good conditions for all workers.

● Job openings for people with learning disabilities does not appear to be influenced by prevailing levels of unemployment. In Ireland for example with 20% unemployment, the Open Road Project succeeded in placing 24 people in 'real jobs' all of whom had been refused a place in sheltered workshops because of the severity of their handicaps.

• Supporting and training a person in the actual workplace has proved more successful than pre-vocational training courses which usually result in the person spending an indeterminate amount of time in segregated settings with little prospect of a move to open employment.

• Recent surveys with school-leavers and attenders at Adult Centres underline the desire of people with learning disabilities to have a job of work. Most have a clear perception of their own capabilities and their job preferences reflect this.

• A growing number of people with learning disabilities in Britain, Europe and America are holding down a job of work, both paid and unpaid, part-time and full-time. The lessons gleaned for these experiences can be used locally.

Strategies for Finding Employers

* Draw up a listing of employment opportunities locally. Drive around industrial estates; walk down High Street listing all the businesses and offices. Consult commercial directories in local libraries.

* Make a list of potential business contacts through colleagues, neighbours, families of people with learning disabilities.

* Exploit the job opportunities within statutory services, especially social service departments, community education and health boards. Often these agencies have a poor record for taking on people with learning disabilities. Use personal contacts to find openings for work experience and paid employment.

* Collate the information in a format which makes it easily accessible, for example the name of person to contact in the business, jobs available, hours of work, pay and so on.

* Develop a business vocabulary. Few staff in services have ever worked in a factory. Beware of disability jargon; keep your messages clear and simple.

* Obtain as much information in advance about the business you are contacting so that you can show that you have done your home-work and you can ask knowledgeable questions.

* Determine clients' preferences and strengths (The Table opposite is taken from a study carried out in the Borders Region of Scotland; p. 14). Use this information to select businesses for initial calls.

* Talks to local Rotary Groups, Chambers of Commerce can increase awareness among employers as will articles in local papers or items on local radio. Provide telephone numbers and addresses for follow-up contacts.

* Organise lunches or exhibitions with personal invitations sent to potential employers. Although not many employers attend, these events can be useful in generating publicity.

Survey of job preferences with 27 people
who have learning disabilities

Job	Could do it	Would Like to do it
Dish-washer	100%	78%
Cook	82%	59%
Domestic	82%	67%
Gardener	70%	48%
Canteen Work	59%	59%
Laundry	52%	33%
Road-sweeper	52%	26%
Store-person	48%	59%
Milkman	44%	30%
Bar-person	41%	33%
Carpenter	41%	37%
Shop Assistant	37%	30%
Farmer	26%	19%

Making Contact with Employers

* Prepare a colour brochure, giving short, snappy information about the placements. It is worth spending money to present a strong image of the project and the people. This can serve a number of uses, for example sending to individual employers; for distribution at meetings etc.

* When approaching businesses aim for an interview with the person responsible for staff appointments. Telephone requests are generally useful.

* Be persistent. This alone may ultimately get you an interview!

* Dress appropriately for interviews. You need to look the part; professional and trustworthy!

* You are 'selling' the abilities of people with learning disabilities. Employers are used to dealing with sales people and they judge the product on your performance! You need to be confident; well-prepared to counter their reservations and well-briefed about the people you are hoping to place. If you do not know the person well, then bring along someone who does. Employers may ask the strangest questions and they expect a definite answer!

* A common mistake is to focus overly on disability. Rather get the employer talking about their business and any particular disabilities they may in getting staff and filling particular jobs.

* Be honest. Employers may seek guarantees which you cannot give. But be clear about the support which you can provide. Have this worked out in detail.

* Be specific. Know in advance what you want from the employer. Ensure that everything is in place so that it can start straightaway if need be.

* Rarely is payment the main issue. Employers are more likely to be concerned about strange behaviours; safety concerns etc.

* Inform employers about the various payments which are available to employers who take on people with disabilities.

* Employers have a social conscience and often this is their prime motivation for agreeing to take a person on your recommendation. Use social justice arguments.

* Even if there are no jobs available at present, ask for a tour of the job-site. As you walk around, point out to the employer

potential jobs which people with learning disabilities could be taught to do. This helps to correct mistaken stereotypes. A tour is also an opportunity to carry out an 'environmental analysis' of the job. Are the staff friendly; how much social integration and support is present; what's the atmosphere like? Your 'gut reaction' may quickly exclude the business from your list!

* If there is a possibility of a placement; suggest that the employer meet the person with learning disabilities; propose a one month trial period.

* Work experience placements should always be time-limited and reviewed regularly, not least as this provides opportunities to review payments.

* If there is little prospect of an immediate placement, then keep a foot in door. *"If you can't get a yes, avoid taking no!"*

* Follow up the interview with a personal letter. You can refer to this correspondence when re-approaching at a later date.

Introducing Workers

* First undertake a detailed analysis of what the job actually entails. This may not square with what the employer tells you about the job, or key steps are left out of their descriptions. In addition, the social aspects of the jobs should be defined; toilets, breaks, lockers etc.

* The service supporter (here called 'job coach') should work on the job for at least a day before bringing the person with learning disabilities (the trainee) into the workplace. This enables them to deal with the queries of co-workers and Shop Stewards.

* The supervisor of the staff should be involved from day one with the trainees, in planning their training and in giving them natural feedback. Supervisors should be encouraged to communicate directly with the trainee and not through the job coach.

* The job coach provides a model for the co-workers as to how they might interact with the trainee. Use their expertise to find ways of adapting jobs to suit the trainees.

* As the placement unfolds, try to identify co-workers who have a particular interest in, or talent for supporting the trainee.

* The goal is to have the job coach withdraw so that the trainee becomes fully integrated into the workforce. Beware of leaving the support for too long that employers, co-workers and trainees become dependent on it. Withdraw by mutual agreement with a phased plan.

* Provide employers with emergency contact numbers but also maintain regular contact through visits and phone calls.

* Employers tend to find trainee's emotional and social problems the hardest to deal with. Support is needed both to prevent and cope with these problems.

* Trainees may give supervisors and co-workers little feedback as to their feelings about the job hence it is important for job supporters to provide this through personal contacts - for example, reactions from families, changes in the person outside of work.

* Most employers prefer to make payments to trainees; these can be graded both in terms of the person's productivity (e.g. their output is about 50% of that of a non-disabled operative) or in terms of the number of hours worked so that their payments does not affect their benefits.

* Use employers and co-workers as advocates with others - through video-recordings, talks, presentations at business events.

Family Attitudes

A common experience among workshop participants was the negative reactions which families often showed to their relative with learning disabilities being placed in open employment. The following recommendations were made as to how this issue might be tackled.

* Family concerns often arise from feelings of protection. Older parents especially need reassurance that the risks are minimised. You need to have these thought through from the parent's perspective. A particular concern with ladies is that they could be exploited sexually.

* Families need support; their concerns are real to them no matter how irrational they appear to us. They need to build up trusted relationships with service workers; preferably through home visits.

* Invite parents to the Day centre so that they can experience at first hand the activities and ethos. The latter can be especially difficult to communicate to parents.

* We need to 'de-institutionalise' parental expectations of services. Moreover day centres are rarely places of work, although this is often how parents refer to them.

* Encourage parental participation in self-travel programmes so that they can see the safeguards and strategy in use. This is often more of a concern that the job placement.

* Use parent meetings to promote the idea of work placements; have parents who have positive experience of this talking to other parents.

* The conflict between parents rights and those of their adult son/daughter needs to be acknowledged and advocated. Involve parents in identifying client needs and planning to meet those needs. Families need to appreciate the reasons underlying our recommendations.

* Press for a one month trial in work placements. The experience can convince more readily than words.

* The threat of lose of benefits may concern low-income families. You need to have accurate and up-to-date information to present to them.

* Should problems arise with placements, handle families with 'kid gloves' so that it can be worked through productively.

* Much of the art of approaching employers applies equally to families.

Service Issues

In this final section, recommendations are made for overcoming some of the obstacles to employment of persons with learning disabilities, encountered in our present service systems.

* Clear policy statements are needed from Social Service Departments and other service providers that employment is one of the service goals.

* Local co-ordination is required among services looking for work placements for this client group - Schools, Colleges, Employment Services etc. Might they 'employ' one person with responsibility for job-finding with service staff providing the job training. Social Service Departments should take a lead in this. Employment goals need to feature in community care plans.

* Training and Enterprise Councils are responsible for employment training in their area. They offer a number of schemes, some with European funding for training people for work.

* Job finding and on-the-job training cannot be carried out by staff who are employed to work in centres. Dedicated staffing is

required for the two functions as they require diverse talents and experiences.

* New types of training opportunities are needed for service staff, for example in selling and marketing.

* Developing sheltered work enterprises has its advantages and disadvantages. Sizeable numbers of people may be placed in jobs of their choosing in the short-term, but sources of secure funding can be difficult to find if the managers do not have the business acumen to sustain the operation. Moreover placements in ordinary jobs are still required in order to provide a through-put of clients.

* A person's level of disability is not a reliable guide to their work performance. Hence 'more able' people may need more support than so-called 'less able' people.

Further Reading

McConkey, R. & McGinley, P. (1992). *Innovations in Employment Training and Work for People with Learning Difficulties*, Chorley, Lisieux Hall Publications.

Moon, M.S. et al. (1990). *Helping Persons with Severe Mental Retardation to Get and Keep Employment - Supported Employment Issues and Strategies* Baltimore, Paul Brookes Publishing

Porterfield, J. & Gathercole, C. (1985). *Employment for people with mental handicap: Progress towards an ordinary working life,* Project paper 55, London, King's Fund Centre.

Walsh, Patricia (1990). *Creating Work Opportunities for Europeans with Mental Handicap*, Chorley, Lisieux Hall Publications.

Survey Findings

Harrison, B. & Tomes, A. (1990). Employers' attitudes to the employment of people with mental handicaps: An empirical study, *Mental Handicap Research,* 3, 196-213.

Levy, J.M. et al (1992). Attitudes of Fortune 500 corporate executives toward the employability of persons with severe disabilities: A national study, *Mental Retardation,* 30, 67-76.

National Development Team (1992). *Supported Employment for People with Learning Disabilities,* Manchester, NDT.
(available from: National Development Team, St Peter's Court, 8, Trumpet Street, Manchester M1 5LW.

Workshop Participants

Pauline Crombie, Rannoch Centre, Edinburgh
Ian Huggan, Lothian Region District Office
Elaine McDonald, Forest View Centre, Stonehaven
Charlie Knox & Elaine Ferguson , Employment Skill Training, Ayr
Linda Reid, Barnardo's Fred Martin Project, Glasgow
Ian Short, Hazeldean Work Resource Centre, Kilwinning
Catriona Wilkinson, Arrol Park, Ayr
Juliet Sheriff & Isobel McIntosh, Lothian Special Needs Employment
Jean Lynch, Hamilton Drive Centre, Elgin
Gordon MacNeish, Annita Reid and Fiona Murray, Clydeville Day
    Centre, Buckie
Jacqueline Robertson, Bonnington Resource Centre, Edinburgh
Hilary Levack, East Lothian Social Work Dept., East Linton
Alan Broad, Wedderburn ATC, Musselburgh
Mark Sprott, Orbiston ATC, Bellshill
Margaret Burns, SSMH, Hamilton
Amanda Carnie, Grindlay Court Centre, Edinburgh
Rhona McNabb, Dudhope Resource Centre, Dundee
Craig Mulley, Kemback Resource Centre, Dundee
Donna Brogan, Peterhead Social Work Department
Jane Fairnie, Cherry Road Centre, Bonnyrigg.

REASSURING NEIGHBOURS

Hostile reactions from neighbours of proposed community developments is one of the most frequently given reasons for educating communities about disability.

Yet opinions are split on whether contact is made with neighbours before or after a residence opens. Some advocate a 'rights' approach with minimal information and consultation with neighbours beforehand. Others argue that residents' integration into the neighbourhood depends on building good relationships and these need to be forged from when the property is acquired. The workshop provided an opportunity to explore these and other issues, such as broader educational strategies aimed at lessening the likelihood of adverse reactions.

The aims of the workshop were:

● To identify good practice when dealing with neighbours of community residences for people with learning disabilities;

● To define the legal requirements for consulting neighbours;

● To develop links between Network members with common interests in this area;

● To explore the role which the Network and its members might play in the development of resource materials for use in educating neighbours.

Our speakers were:

✿ Hilary Patrick, Legal Adviser to the Scottish Association for Mental Health and author of *'Mental Health Law in Scotland'*.

✿ Philip Russell, Development Officer, ELCAP, East Lothian
  (A voluntary organisation providing community housing)

✿ Kevin Hutchins, Disability Project, Grampian Social Work Department, Stonehaven.

To Consult or Not to Consult?

In legal terms, 'consultation' implies more than informing or notifying neighbours. It means talking to people before a decision is reached and allowing their views to influence your own. This effectively means being prepared to give neighbours the right to veto the project should they not approve it.

Service providers are most reluctant to do this, for the following reasons:

☐ If given the opportunity, neighbours would likely object; thereby jeopardising the whole policy of community housing. Experiences in North America appear to bear this out. Upwards of 50% of proposed community housing fails to open due to neighbourhood opposition.

☐ Nobody has the right to choose their neighbours. It is therefore stigmatising if this has to occur for certain groups. Anti-discriminatory legislation prohibits this happening for people from ethnic minorities. There is no similar legislation covering people with disabilities.

Although this has led some providers into adopting a 'low-profile' approach of opening the house without telling anyone outside of the service the use to which it will be put; other providers feel that the giving of information to neighbours is inevitable.

Services should avoid using the word 'consultation' unless they are prepared to genuinely concede to neighbours demands. Adverse reactions are fuelled if the consultation is exposed as a sham. Government guidance also needs to differentiate between a requirement to exchange information and hold discussions and a requirement for consultation. In particular, the Scottish Office Circular (1989) to Health Boards on consultation with neighbours, needs urgent revision. Fortunately this is underway. The draft of the new guidance states:

In all contacts with neighbours .. it is important to make absolutely clear that "consultations" at this stage involve exchanging information and listening to views: they do not give local residents a right to choose their neighbours.

Legal requirements to inform

In certain circumstances, there are legal requirements to inform neighbours.

■ Applications for planning permission and/or to building control for adaptations to the property;

■ In public sector housing, some District Councils oblige project managers to consult with Tenant's Associations or Community Councils before new supported accommodation can be allocated. However the legal status of this requirement is not clear.

Legal Obstacles

The title deeds of private houses often state that it will be used as a private dwelling for family use. Solicitors should check the deeds on prospective houses as neighbours could lodge an objection on the grounds that a group home would not be in keeping with the deeds.

However in recent cases in Scotland and Kent, this argument was not upheld on the grounds that it ran counter to the wider public policy of care in the community. Another line of defence is the imprecision of the term 'family'.

In Scots Law, the Feudal Superior can specify conditions which supersede the title deeds to the house. Superiority can be retained when land is sold for building, or it can be bought. This device could be used to proscribe the opening of a group home although it can be challenged in law. Equally buying the Superiority with the title deeds of the property prevents this occurring.

In new residential developments, the title deeds may allow neighbours to enforce conditions against one another. This usually covers issues such as maintaining gardens and parking caravans but could be used to prevent group homes opening in an estate.

Finally, some neighbours have resorted to legal challenges to existing homes on the grounds of 'nuisance' such as excess noise which makes it intolerable for them to live in their home. Such claims can still be made, even when the person moved into the area in full knowledge of the home's existence. As yet, there is little case law relating to such claims.

Agencies can insure against the costs of defending legal actions.

Informing Neighbours

Diverse opinions exist on the degree and detail of information which is given to neighbours and on how best this might be done. Particular concerns centre around confidentiality of information about prospective residents.

Services are advised to develop a policy on informing neighbours and to regularly update this in the light of experience. This helps to ensure a consistent approach among service personnel; especially if the policy defines the staff who have responsibility for informing neighbours; it provides a definition of 'neighbours' (e.g. the people on either side of a detached or semi-detached house; people sharing a common stair) and outlines how approaches are to be made. Sample policies are available from ELCAP and Grampian Social Work Department (see p. 106).

The reasons given for informing neighbours are that:

● it is unrealistic, in small towns especially, that neighbours will not find out about the proposal, for instance, from people selling the house.

● rumours can increase fears and anxieties. Speaking to the people directly gives them more accurate information about the organisation's policies and practices and provides an opportunity to counter misinformation (see below).

● it makes life easier for the residents moving in. Neighbourhood surveys suggest a majority of neighbours are willing to meet with the residents but they are unsure as to whether or not this would be welcome.

Contacting neighbours

The growing body of experience at informing neighbours has yet to be matched by systematic research into which approaches are the most effective. However some consensus is emerging on what is *generally* effective; the proviso being that every community is a unique combination of people, traditions and concerns, whose reactions are not fully predictable.

Hence the first piece of advice is never become complacent, always read the signals and respond to the reactions.

The second key advice is that agencies must spell out the reasons why they want to, or feel they need to inform neighbours. This will help clarify the methods and style they use.

Public meetings are best avoided. Notice of a meeting will give opponents a chance to mobilise. Those with concerns are the most likely people to attend whereas those who have no strong feelings will stay away, or if they do come, they could be won over by the rhetoric of the articulate. Hence at public meetings, service personnel are invariably put on the defensive. Moreover the neighbours take up positions from which it is hard to back down without losing face.

Nevertheless some statutory agencies may be obliged to hold such meetings.   In these instances careful preparation of the presentation is required; including the presence of vocal allies in the audience. A review of the impact of such meetings would help to clarify their usefulness.

Open Days are questionable They are not appropriate once the residents move in and yet without them neighbours can only meet the staff and admire the decoration. The uptake of invitations is low and critics of the project are more likely to stay away.

The preferred approach is face-to-face meetings with neighbours in their own homes. For example, one agency organised a team of staff so that all the neighbours were visited on the same evening. In this way, everyone heard at the same time and unfounded rumours were prevented from spreading.

ELCAP uses the following strategy:

♦ Once a property has been purchased or leased, ELCAP write to prospective neighbours (see earlier definition) offering a meeting with a member of staff. Around two in five neighbours take up this offer.

♦ The same member of staff - the Development Worker - visits all neighbours. Hence he not only brings a consistency to the dealings with neighbours but can build up particular expertise in handling neighbour's concerns and reactions.

♦ The neighbours are informed about the project's aims and objectives and how it will operate, e.g. staffing. Time is taken to elicit and listen to neighbours' concerns. Reassurances are given by citing local experiences. Most people can be talked round to giving the project a try. If neighbours want to have further discussions, they are given the names and addresses of the organisation's office-bearers.

♦ ELCAP do not give neighbours a veto on whether the project proceeds. This is made clear in all their dealings as is their intention to fight any legal moves.

♦ If antagonism proves excessive, the organisation may abandon the project for the sake of the prospective tenants. This has not happened as yet and the concern would be that a precedent would be set that could jeopardise other schemes.

A general rule of thumb is to be open and approachable. Ensure all neighbours have the name, address and phone number of a person who they can contact for further information.

Concerns and confidentiality

The most commonly expressed concerns of neighbours are:

- ✪ Staff cover; lack of consultation; noise and disturbance; behaviour of residents;
- ✪ Residents interfering with children and children teasing residents; parking;
- ✪ House prices dropping (see p. 105).

Although complainants may not be amenable to rational argument; they should be given the facts and figures. For example, property prices do not fall; people with learning disabilities are no more likely than other adults to assault children. (Unfortunately, the evidence usually has to be drawn from North American studies but comparable data could be collected by local agencies).

Another source of evidence is to contrast the actual experiences of residents living adjacent to group homes with their concerns before the house opened or compared to similar areas with no home (see further reading).

A possible danger though is that reassurances to neighbours could mean breaching resident's confidentiality. The Scottish Office Code of Practice on Confidentiality of Personal Health Information which is binding on voluntary as well as statutory agencies states that personal health information should only be disclosed on a 'need-to-know' basis or with the consent (preferably written) of the patient.

Hence, information about prospective residents should be couched in general terms and staff should avoid discussing particular people, especially those who may be known already to neighbours. Assurances can be given that problems will be dealt with; for instance by giving the name of contact person.   However no guarantees can be offered that neighbours will have a trouble-free existence from each other.

Another safeguard is for the person meeting the neighbours to have little or no direct contact with the prospective residents and he/she is less likely to inadvertently disclose confidential information.

Neighbours' concerns are most effectively addressed by meeting the residents. Hence a common experience is for opposition to die away after the residents move in. Sometimes the original critics become the strongest supporters.

Opposition is minimised if the project gets started with the minimum of notice.

Building Community Support

Waiting until houses are about to open before informing the public is to court opposition. Broader educational initiatives can create a more positive climate of opinion and make it easier for people to espouse new styles of services when little or no personal threat is involved. Among the strategies which have proved successful in local communities and neighbours are:

* Stories in local papers with headlines such as 'Neighbours welcome new project for people with disabilities'. These help to counteract the more negative reports of opposition and give prominence to your supporters (see p. 107).

* Informing community councillors, district and regional councillors of your plans and proposals and getting their support (see p. 119). Their participation in the organisation's management or advisory committees is also useful. Opposers are likely to approach them and their objections need to be forestalled at this level.

* Making contact with influential people in the community such as church leaders, doctors, newspaper reporters to give them your 'side of the story' so that they are briefed if approached by opposers; they can scotch rumours and may even mobilise support in your favour.

* Letters to the local papers from neighbours of existing properties who can counter opposer's arguments.

* Talks and meetings with local groups such as Rotary, Lunch Clubs, Resident's Association to explain the rationale behind community care and engage their support when there is no immediate 'threat' to them personally. It could then be harder for them to oppose a project at a future date. Video presentations which promote the 'rights' of people with disabilities have been found to be effective.

* Promotional videos in which neighbour's of existing residences gave their opinions; talking honestly about any reservations they had before the home opened and how their concerns were dispelled.

* Ensuring that existing homes are not open to criticism, e.g. tidy gardens; well maintained frontage and considerate parking of cars etc.

* Employing local people to work in the community residences. This can counter misinformation and helps the residents integrate socially as they meet the staff's family and friends. However confidentiality needs to be stressed.

* Encouraging people with learning disabilities to use public amenities, such as buses, supermarkets, libraries and swimming pools, so that the community has opportunities to meet them.

* Get to know the local community and keep a high profile of your agency in the community.

* Community care plans should contain clear statements about the need for housing in the community and the benefits for the recipients.

* As more community houses open, adverse reactions seem to decrease as communities become accustomed to this new style of service and the 'folk wisdom' accumulates that certain concerns are unfounded.

FAMILIARITY BREEDS SUPPORT

Avoiding Conflict

Another pertinent strategy is for services to choose the neighbourhoods more carefully in which they propose to open a residence. A growing body of research has identified the characteristics of neighbourhoods in which opposition is more likely to be encountered.

> * The neighbours are 'incomers' to the area; people who have recently bought property
> * Retirement 'estates'; with people over 60 who have had little past contact with people who have a learning disability
> * Articulate professionals, who may have some marginal involvement with the client group; e.g. GPs, health board officials.
> * Leafy middle-class suburbs with a preponderance of owner-occupied, single family dwellings.

Experience on the ground, suggests that the most vehement opposition has come from neighbourhoods which meet two or more of these criteria. The solution perhaps is to look elsewhere if at all possible rather than risk protracted conflict and the social isolation of the residents in that neighbourhood.

Another consideration is the number of special housing projects already present in an area and whether the creation of another runs to risk of creating a 'ghetto' into which non-handicapped people will not want to move. A suggested rule is that the number of people with disabilities in a neighbourhood should not exceed the number found in the average population, namely one in a hundred.

Resident selection Equally, certain residents may give rise to legitimate complaints from neighbours. For example, excessive noise can be more easily tolerated in a detached house, than in flats or terrace housing. Better forward planning of housing to meet the particular needs of residents could also prevent unnecessary conflict. Indeed the needs of certain people with learning disabilities may make it inappropriate for them to reside in ordinary community settings, for instance those prone to violent outbursts.

Good Neighbours

Maintaining good relationships with neighbours often requires no special effort; other than following the customs and practices of that neighbourhood. For instance, not being overly friendly if neighbours merely pass the time of day with one another but equally taking your turn at hosting parties and barbecues if these are common practice.

In some areas, residents and staff have gone out of their way to be of assistance to their neighbours, for instance, by cutting the grass for an elderly neighbour, letting people have access to their telephone.

Problems can arise though in the best planned schemes. Two of the most commonly reported are:

✿ *Older children and young adults teasing and threatening the residents.*
The end terrace houses on Council Estates, close to public paths, seem to be particularly prone to gangs of youths congregating. Police involvement and contact with parents may have some effect

but more successful are schemes which educate the young people about the effect they have on their victims (such as is used in school-based approaches to bullying) and those which try to engage the young people in community development schemes. In extreme cases of teasing the residents have had to be relocated.

✿ *Neighbours wanting a particular resident moved.*
Complaints need to be dealt with promptly by the project manager and facts established. Within the code of confidentiality, outside expert opinion can be sought. Reassurances can be given about staffing and supervision. Follow-up meetings need to be arranged to maintain contact with neighbours.

A house in the community does not imply a home for life. Group homes may move to other areas if the needs of residents change or the characteristics of the neighbourhood change. In these early days of community care, the temptation is to think that a move means a defeat whereas it can be a normal part of community life.

Future Directions

○ Clarification is urgently needed on the apparently contradictory guidance which different sections of the Scottish Office have issued to Health Boards and Social Work Departments.

○ Service agencies providing community housing, need to have an explicit policy on contact with neighbours and to monitor the effect which this has on neighbour's reactions. A common policy across agencies would be in everyone's interests as would a documented body of knowledge about the strategies which have proved to be effective.

○ Local community care plans should promote the need for housing in the community; dispel unfounded fears and promote the rights of tenants with special needs.

○ Service planners need to become better informed about the characteristics of the local communities into which they inject residences and more discerning about matching prospective residents to communities.

Further Reading

Community Care and Consultation: A report by the Scottish Mental Health Foundation (1992). Available from: Scottish Association for Mental Health, 38, Gardner's Crescent, Edinburgh, EH3 8DQ

Janicki, M.P. et al. (1988). *Community residences for people with developmental disabilities: Here to stay,* Baltimore, Paul Brookes Publishing.

Survey Findings

Leyin, A. (1988). What shall we tell the neighbours?, *Mental Handicap*, 16, 11-15.

McConkey, R. et al (1993). Neighbours' reaction to community services: Contrasts before and after services open in their locality, *Mental Handicap Research*, 2, 131-141.

Pittock, F. & Potts, M. (1988). Neighbourhood attitudes to people with a mental handicap, *British Journal of Mental Subnormality*, 34, 35-46.

Roycroft, P. & Hames, A. (1990). Local objections to community-based houses: Factors for consideration, *Mental Handicap*, 18, 11-14.

Ryan, C.S. & Coyne, A. (1985). Effects of group homes on neighbourhood property values, *Mental Retardaion,* 23, 241-245.

See also p. 13 in this volume

Contact Addresses

ELCAP, Woodbine Cottage, West Loan, Prestonpans, East Lothian EH32 9NU

Social Work Department, Grampian Regional Council, Woodhill House, Westburn Road, Aberdeen AB9 2LU

Workshop Participants

Tracey Sanderson, Edinburgh Priority Unit
Ian Collins, Edinburgh Priority Unit
Pat Turnbull, Community Development Project, Dumfries
Stan Phillips, Community Nurse, Dundee
Paul McArthur, Key Housing, Glasgow
John Redwood, L'Arche, Inverness

DEALING WITH THE MEDIA

The media has an important role in educating communities about learning disabilities.

First, they can project more positive images of people with learning disabilities; particularly their abilities, emotions and integration in the life of the community.

Second, the media can help with the promotion of events or schemes that will bring the public into contact with people who have learning disabilities.

Third, news and feature articles can make the public more informed about learning disabilities and new styles of services - community housing; employment placements etc.

Our guest at the workshop was Dorothy Grace Elder, a freelance journalist and broadcaster with extensive experience in the Scottish media. She has taken a particular interest in disability and worked for Scottish Television as a script-writer on this topic.

Workshop participants from various parts of Scotland, contributed their experiences and knowledge from local media contacts. Information has also been gleaned from a number of publications which are listed at the end of this section.

Reflections on Media Contacts

"A journalist shall only mention a person's race, colour, creed, illegitimacy, marital status (or lack of it), gender, sexual orientation or disability if this information is strictly relevant. A journalist shall neither originate nor process material which encourages discrimination on any of the above-mentioned grounds. "
Code of Conduct: Clause 10: National Union of Journalists.

It is important to remember that any fund-raising campaign is really 'successful' only if it both brings in the money and presents a positive image of people with mental handicaps" Ann Shearer.

The need for justice and pity should always be stressed... Patronising language should not be used. Words like 'plucky', 'courage', bravery or tragedy' creates an image of people with disabilities as pitiable martyrs. Spastics Society

Avoid describing people with Down's Syndrome as "victim of" or "suffering from". Instead use the phrases "someone who has ... or a person with Down's Syndrome. Down's Syndrome Association

The best headlines (in job adverts) were those which were trying to put over some positive and eye-catching messages about the aims and objectives of a particular service. So there were advertisements whose headlines read: ... "encouraging independence" or 'Heard of Life-Sharing?. Alison Wertheimer

Try to ensure that the Press quotes the views of people with learning difficulties wherever possible. A commitment to consumerism and self-advocacy means standing back and letting people with learning difficulties speak for themselves. Alison Wertheimer

There is no such thing as a neutral image of a person who has a mental handicap. Unless it is deliberately made positive, people will see it as confirming their negative preconceptions - whether that is intended or not" Ann Shearer

People with disabilities rarely get the opportunity to work in the media. Yet no-one can represent people with disabilities better than they themselves.

Starting Points

Before you start trying to improve the way the media portrays
people with learning disabilities, make sure that your own house is
in order! Do your own publications use appropriate language and
do your services offer positive and valued images.

Have more than one person in your group or organisation to deal
with the press and see that they are well clued up.

The staff in PR Departments of Health Boards and Social Work
departments may need to be educated about learning disabilities.
Insist that you check any releases which they send out on your
behalf. Try to have press calls handled by a person who knows
the 'story' rather than by a PR representative.

You can pay PR companies to arrange publicity for you. The cost
may not justify the coverage.

You don't have to wait for members of the press to call you. If
you have something you want to publicise - and you think it is
really newsworthy - seize the initiative and write to the
newspapers.

Do not be over-awed by the media. They are ordinary men and
women doing a job.

Journalists are likely to share the same prejudices and fears about
people with learning disabilities as some other members of society.
You need to make time to educate them!

Try to ensure that the press quotes the views of people with
learning disabilities whenever possible. Make a point of
introducing reporters to people with learning disabilities and give

them time to talk. Make proper introductions; forenames and surnames.

Get to know the members of the Press you want to work with, make personal contacts, take the trouble to find out what stories interest them - but remember don't start preaching. Journalists will want to make up their own mind.

You could invite editors and sub-editors to a social event to build personal contacts. This will help you to brief them about your work. Present them with copies of some of the booklets on media and disability (see p. 116).

It's easy to campaign against bad, inaccurate and biassed media coverage but remember that positive feedback can also be a force for change. A personal letter to the editor thanking him or her for good coverage is always appreciated.

All of the foregoing points should help to improve the quality and not just the quantity of coverage given to learning disabilities. The old adage that any publicity is better than none does not apply to people with disabilities when we want to change the public's stereotypes and prejudices rather than confirm them!

Warn your telephone operators about any special publicity so that they can handle any enquiries well briefed. You don't want your efforts at publicity to be wasted!

Ground Rules

Always be honest when dealing with journalists. If you don't tell the truth you will lose credibility with the press.

Journalists often work on a tight schedule. Be prepared to give quick answers and if you promise to call them back by a certain time; then keep your promise. If you don't, you may find that they do not bother to contact you again.

Unless you specifically say that you are 'speaking off the record', then the reporter will presume that they can quote you! Beware of unguarded comments.

You can issue a press release, 'embargoed' to a specific date and time. The press will make no mention of it until after that deadline has passed but it gives them time to prepare the story. However use embargoes selectively. It is much better to label the release *'for immediate publication'*. This gives the press the freedom to use it whenever they wish.

You can send the same press release to as many different papers and radio stations as you want. Only one or two may take up the story but be prepared to set up a 'press conference' at the event if there is a great deal of interest. This is simply a time and place when all the journalists can be briefed and have a chance to ask questions. Following this, individual interviews can be arranged.

Headlines are decided by the sub-editor. There is not much that you can do to influence the headline other than providing a phrase in the second or third paragraph of the release that might 'leap out'.

Always give the press at least one week's notice of any event (preferably two) so that they can enter it in their news diaries. Then follow up two days to go with a call to the news desk to see if they are coming.

Collectively local papers throughout the country can give you more coverage than big dailies. Never ignore their power - they are often short of material. In your press release you can stress the local links.

Press Releases

Prepare clearly worded press releases. Two pages are recommended. The first giving factual details - exact locations, timing, names. This should brief and punchy. The second page can spell out more details.

Use plain everyday language in your releases. Avoid jargon, long descriptions and ambiguity.

Include two quotes from named people which the press can use in their reports.

Make sure that your release mentions photo opportunities that will be available

Include the names of TWO people which reporters can contact along with their day and evening phone numbers.

The press thrives on human interest. Stress people's individuality rather than emphasising that they are part of a group ("the handicapped"). Do your own research carefully beforehand so that you can answer any queries from reporters.

Send your press releases not only to the news desk but also to individual journalists with a particular health/social brief, or women's pages, health slots etc. Address them to the "women's editor" or deputy.

Get central address for newspaper chains, e.g. Scottish and Universal have some 15 different titles. One release sent to them will reach 15 editors.

Choose the day you send out releases - avoid Friday.

Photographs

Stories on the popular press are picture-led. Often they are looking for 'happy, happy' pictures to counterbalance the more common horrific ones!

Set up photo-opportunities which have people doing interesting things. Line-ups of people are not very eye-catching! Offer various alternative scenes to the photographer.

Present people with handicaps in situations which exaggerate neither their abilities ("Man wins 50 yard walking race") nor their disabilities.

Try to have the people with disabilities in ordinary settings and mixing with non-disabled people in shared activities which are age-appropriate and in ways which others would find acceptable to themselves.

Call the paper two days before the event to see if they are sending along their own photographer.

You can arrange to have your own black and white photos taken for distribution to the press. Do not use amateurs. Have a variety of pictures taken in different shapes so that editors have a choice. Supply detailed captions of people in the pictures - giving full names of everyone. Send in 7x5 inch glossy prints. You can ask to have the pictures returned.

Avoid having the photo too cluttered with faces forward and a plain background so that the people stand out.

The press like a 'celebrity' in pictures.

Other Press Contacts

Never forget the simple value of a reader's letter to the Editor from your organisation, or as a private individual. This way you can stress addresses and telephone numbers which might be left out of reports.

Response should be made to any negative press. You can organise a letter-writing campaign to give a contrary viewpoint. For example, reactions to protests by neighbours of a prospective group home.

Organisations and individuals can make use of the Press Council's complaints system if they feel coverage infringes people's rights and dignity.

You could offer to contribute to regular features which the paper runs, such as diary pages.

Explore the possibility of the paper running a feature article linked to national issues but giving the local perspective; e.g. changes in benefits. Or you may offer to provide a series of short articles along the lines of Facts about disability.

Job advertisements which human service organisations place in papers and magazines are also an advert about them and the people they serve. Do these 'ads' carry positive images?

Local Radio

Many of the foregoing points apply equally to news and features items on local radio. Contact the presenters and/or producers of individual programmes as well as the news-desk and their reporters. The Radio Times will give names of producers.

Provide the radio station with the names of good 'chatter-boxes' who they could invite on to the programme or contact for comment.

You might suggest topics for phone-ins to the radio station; giving names of people who could be in the studio and arrange for some callers.

You can approach producers with ideas for a programme or series of programme. Spell out the aims; target listeners; who could take part; where recordings could be made etc. Follow-up your letter with a request to meet.

Community Press

Finally, don't forget the many opportunities for publicity and information spreading offered by community newsletters produced by Resident Associations, Churches and Clubs.

Further Reading

Think Positive: Advice on presenting people with mental handicap
by Ann Shearer. Available from:
    International League of Societies for Persons with
      Mental handicap,
    24, Ave. Louise, boite 17,
    B-1050 BRUSSELS, Belgium

Improving communications about people with disabilities
Available from -
    United Nations
    Division for Economic and Social Information
    Department of Public Information
    New York, NY 10017, USA

*According to the Papers*and *Images by Appointment: A review of
advertising for staff in services for people with learning difficulties.*
Both publications by Alison Wertheimer; Available from:
    VIA
    12a Maddox Street
    London W1R 9PL

Media Matters - Social Work, the Press and Broadcasting
by Ann Fry; Available from:
    Community Care
    Reed Business Publications
    Carew House
    Wallngton, Surrey SM6 OD6

Talk about Disability
Available from:
    The Spastics Society
    12, Park Crescent
    London W1N 4EQ

It's About Disability
Available from:
   National Union of Journalists
   314, Grays Inn Road
   London WC1X 8DP

Hitting the Headlines: A practical guide to the media: by Stephen White et al. Published by the British Psychological Society, Leicester, 1993

They aren't in the brief: Advertising and people with disabilities by S. Scott-Parker. Published by the King's Fund Centre, 1989

Workshop Participants

Julian Brooke, Psychological Services, Kirkcaldy
Pauline Crombie, Rannoch Centre, Edinburgh
Billy Doherty, Tayside Social Work, Dundee
Michael Duff, Tayside Social Work , Dundee
Fiona Hardie, Volunteer Development Scotland Project
   Strathmartine Hospital
Margaret Hurcombe, FAIR, Edinburgh
Linda Kerr, Information Officer, SSMH
Brenda McCrae, Coatbridge College and Toryglen Centre, Glasgow
David McLean, Alpha Project, Cumbernauld
May McLean, Toryglen Resource Centre, Glasgow
Stan Phillips, Community Nursing, Strathmartine Hospital,
   Dundee
Philip Russell, ELCAP, East Lothian
Valerie Tough, Information Unit, SSMH

EDUCATING LOCAL POLITICIANS AND OFFICIALS

The need to educate politicians and officials had been a recurring theme in the early workshops and consultations carried out by the Network. With the advent of community care initiatives it was all the more vital that decision-makers and service planners were aware of the particular needs of people with learning disabilities.

... 'POLITICAL QUESTION TIME'...

The aims of the workshop were:

● To identify strategies for educating and influencing local politicians and officials about issues to do with learning disabilities;

● To share experiences and develop links among Network members with common interests in this topic;

● To explore the role which the Network and its members might play in the development of resource materials and guidelines for educating local politicians.

Our speakers were:

✡ Maria Fyfe MP, Member for Glasgow Maryhill
  and Labour Spokesperson for Health in Scotland.

✡ Cllr. Nan Burnett, Chair of the Social Work Committee,
  Borders Regional Council

✡ Norman Dunning, Director of Enable
  (formerly Scottish Society for Mental Handicap)

✡ Molly Downie, Secretary, Lothian Branch of Enable

The content of the guide was further developed in discussion with the participants; drawing on their past experiences and getting their recommendations for action.

The Issues

The group listed the issues which politicians and officials need to be informed about and on which action was required in order to meet the diverse needs of people with learning disabilities and their carers. This list is not meant to be exhaustive but rather provides a focus around which representations can be made.

   * Funding for community housing

   * The need for respite care and the different styles of provision
     which could be made.

   * Services which meet the needs of people rather than fitting
     people into what is already available.

   * Information about the help which is available locally

* Education for young children with special needs;
   options available

* Post school provision

* Employment training

* Benefit system - eligibility criteria; restoring benefits
   if circumstances change; disincentives in the system.

* Availability of transport, especially if people require
   special therapy.

* Clarifying the rights to service of adult persons with
   learning disabilities.

Contacting Officials

Personal contacts with officials and civil servants should be easy to arrange. Increasingly their job is to deal directly with consumers. Particular issues are likely to be allocated to designated officials within Government Departments. If you want to make contact with them you could:

* contact officials in local authorities or health boards who may be able to give you contact names;

* telephone the information section of the Department or the Scottish Office (031 556 8400);

* write to the Secretary of State outlining the issue and asking advice on who you might meet;

* ask your local MP to obtain the information for you if the foregoing steps have yielded no result.

When meeting with officials it is equally important to listen to their views as well as presenting your own. In particular, note the difficulties they raise. You may be able to counter these during the meeting and in follow-up correspondence and future meetings.

It is vital to get the officials on board with you; politicians invariably follow their recommendations.

If you feel you are not getting a fair deal from officials you can:

* contact media and outline your complaints;

* contact your MP who can make an approach on your behalf.

Contacting Your Local MP

MPs are your representative; do not feel that they will be uninterested in the issues which concern you. Although busy people, a key feature of the job is contact with constituents. You might invite them to AGMs and any special events you organise.

MPs often have constituency offices through which they can be contacted and they may hold regular 'surgeries' in the area when they can meet people.

You can also write to them at the House of Commons, London.

In approaching MPs; give a clear outline of the issue and what response you wish from the member.

At election time, prospective candidates can be approached regarding their views on specific issues. Sympathetic candidates might be persuaded to mention the issue in their speeches and election literature.

Influencing MPs

Lobbying MPs has become big business but often the most effective lobbies are conducted in a low-key manner. Banner-waving, demonstrations may get publicity but their effectiveness is dubious.

MPs are not likely to be well informed about disability issues. You need to present them with basic facts and figures. Also personal stories are effective; for instance the practical difficulties faced by carers.

Some points to bear in mind when planning to lobby MPs.

* Letters to MP are more effective if they are written individually (postcards or pre-printed letters have little effect) and if they are well informed and recount direct experiences.

* Give the MPs plenty of notice if you wish to meet them.

* Choose your day and time carefully; take advice from parliamentarians.

* Find a sympathetic MP who will book meeting rooms for you and help to get you past the crowds at the entrance.

* Target MPs who are known to be, or who are likely to be opposed to your views and spend most time with them rather than with those MPs who are already sympathetic to your cause. Write in advance to request a meeting.

* Try to arrange a photo opportunity; then there is increased likelihood that the media will show an interest in the meeting.

* Prepare your arguments in advance of the meeting and spell out the commitments you expect from the MPs.

* Join forces with similar organisations or come together under an 'umbrella' lobby (see later).

* At election time; candidates can be asked questions at public meetings. During the last General Election, ENABLE drafted six questions which members were encouraged to raise with local candidates either on the doorstep or at public meetings.

Lobbying is as much an art as a science. Campaigns which are conducted with flair and style are more likely to be noticed while the scientific element comes from being able to learn from one's mistakes. But a lot gets done simply through sheer persistence

HOW MPs CAN HELP

You could expect various forms of help from MPs.

* They could ask a parliamentary question. Written questions are useful for extracting information from Government Departments. Oral questions can be followed by supplementaries and these present an opportunity to discover Government plans, priorities and future policies.

* The workings of every Government Department is now monitored by a Select Committee of Parliament. You can write to members of the Committee outlining the issues. Well researched materials are especially helpful to members. Likewise if you wish to make representations on a bill which is going through Parliament, members on the Standing Committee can be sent briefing notes along with suggestions for new clauses and amendments.

* MPs can put down an Early Day motion on which debate is not permitted but this device is a useful way of gaining publicity especially if the motion is signed by a large number of MPs.

* Members may also be able to raise a Private Member's Bill. Again their value is more in generating publicity unless the Government is enthusiastic about the issue.

* In the run up to an election, you could lobby for an issue to be taken up as party policy and for commitments to be made in the manifesto.

Local Government - A Councillor's viewpoint

Many of the foregoing points are just as relevant to local councillors and officials. But remember there are many more of them than there are MPs and Civil Servants!

Your District and Regional Council will supply a full list of the names and addresses of all councillors and the membership of the various committees such as Social Work and Housing.

Members can be contacted by letter with follow up phone calls and meetings.

Some tips on dealing with councillors.

* local politicians of whatever party hue are as likely to have the same prejudices, misunderstandings and fears about 'mental handicap' as the average member of the public.

* councillors will have their own priority issues for their area - be it housing, unemployment. Try to link your issues with their's.

* politicians are dependent on others for information. They appreciate having good information on which to base their decisions. For instance, a survey of carers undertaken by a local Branch of Enable highlighted the need for respite care provision in the Borders Region and enabled the Social Work Committee to obtain the necessary resources. Information from other parts of the country as well as from countries can also prove helpful to them.

* the confrontational approach should be reserved for times when nothing else seems to have worked. Success is more likely to come from persuasion; the 'drip-drip' rather than the 'bull-doze' principle!

* give councillors the opportunity to meet people at first-hand and see the outcomes of positive work. Arrange for service-users to meet Councillors and Committees as they are particularly keen to have their reactions. Invitations can be sent to Open Days and special events.

* councillors are busy people who need to use their time effectively. From your contacts try to find out what they have found (or would find helpful). Try to meet these needs in future contacts.

* take up opportunities offered for consultation. For example, community care plans are open for annual comment.

* newsletters and house magazines can be sent to councillors and copies left in council offices and meeting rooms for members to read between meetings.

It can take a long time to affect change; councillors have no magic wand but you can legitimately ask what plans they are making and for when!

Arranging deputations

A common way of lobbying councillors is by arranging for a deputation of two or three people to meet with one councillor or with a group of councillors. Deputations can also ask to address a Council Committee such as Social Work and may even be able to address the full Council.

Tips for arranging a deputation

* Find out about the councillors in advance; particularly the commitments they made in their election literature;

* You might sit in the public gallery at council meetings to familiarise yourself with the room and the routines.

* Some councillors could be invited to attend a meeting of the group. You could use this opportunity to prepare for the deputation.

* Prepare carefully; identify the main issues and points you wish to make. Check out your facts and have them written down. Allocate issues to the different members of the deputation.

* Go early, at least 15 minutes beforehand. Ensure the officials who introduces you to the group has the correct information about you.

* Address the chair person. Keep your presentation succinct - get quickly to the point as they are busy people.

* Be prepared for questions, they can be fired at you from all directions.

* Do not be put off by people getting up and leaving during the meeting; this can be normal practice.

* If you feel that the councillors are not taking you seriously you might remind them that it was your votes that put them there and you expect their support!

* Be careful on whose behalf you are speaking. Distinguish when you are giving a personal opinion and when you are outlining a group's viewpoint.

Organising an Effective Lobby

Lobbies and deputations are more likely to be effective if they have the backing of some form of organisation. This might be an existing group such as Enable or one which has come together for a specific purpose. The advantages of organisational support would be:

☐ Widen influence
☐ Shared experiences
☐ Brings together knowledge and practical skills
☐ Enables policies to be refined through discussion and debate
☐ Tasks can be shared
☐ Resources can become available
☐ Provides continuity over time.

Influencing policy

Defining policy is like describing a jelly! Policies come in all shapes, sizes and colours. Worse still, policies can change when squeezed!

However policies can determine how resources are spent and may unwittingly disadvantage people with disabilities. In trying to influence policy, here are some points to bear in mind:

* Where does the existing policy come from? Is it framed in legislation? Does it come from Government Regulation (this is quicker to change) or from Government Advice (which has no legislative basis)? Or it is merely custom and practice?

* Clarify what changes are desirable. Check out the arguments supporting your view. Assemble necessary facts and figures and personal examples.

* Guess what the opposers of change might say and counter their views. Think of any obstacles to change or contingencies which might arise from change and try to illustrate how adverse effects could be countered.

* Talk to officials before going public. They invariably will present you with a polite and considered response.

* Find allies with other agencies, gain the support of politicians.

* Find people with expertise when it comes to legal issues or generating publicity.

* The media can prove useful but this can be a double-edged sword. For example, your position might be misrepresented.

Workshop Participants

Katriona Scally, Disability Awareness Unit, Bathgate
Madge Irving, Arrol Park, Ayr
Ian Hood, Action Group, Edinburgh
Gillian Bartrop, Community Education Special Needs Team, Alloa
Irene Frail, Dunfermline
Margaret Duncan, Dunfermline
Bob McCallum, Enable, Glasgow
Derek Bank, Dumfries and Galloway Health Board
Irene Whitefield, Annan
Margaret Gruber, Archdiocese of Glasgow Social Services
Monique Carr, Archdiocese of Glasgow Social Services
Jessie Harrigan, Archdiocese of Glasgow Social Services

LINKING WITH CHURCHES

Although church membership has fallen in recent years, churches still retain a unique role in our society. Larger churches offer a range of activities at little or no cost to people of differing ages and sex. Often these events are both regular and local and provide opportunities for social networks to develop and friendships to be formed. Sunday Services and other religious events provide opportunities for clients' spiritual needs to be met. For all these reasons, links with churches must feature in our community networks.

The aims of the workshop were:

- To identify good practice when linking people with learning disabilities to local churches;

- To define the support and help which members of churches might need;

- To develop links between Network members with common interests in this area;

Our speakers were:

✪ Brian Kelly, Co-ordinator of Training,
        Brothers of Charity Services, Lancashire.

✪ Rev. Janet MacMahon, Chaplain, Southern General Hospital,
        Glasgow (formerly Research and Development Officer for
        the Church of Scotland's *One in a Hundred* Project).

✪ Margaret Hume, formerly Church Liaison Officer,
        Social Work Department, Tayside Regional Council.

The content of this guide was further developed in discussion with the participants; drawing on their past experiences and getting their recommendations for action.

NB. The workshop participants limited their suggestions to Christian Churches as they had little experience of working with other faiths.

What You Need to Know about Churches

* No two churches are alike! Churches vary in so many ways - by denomination; history and traditions; their forms of worship; range of social activities provided; their decision-making structures and of course in the personalities of the leaders and members. Even two churches of the same denomination within the same town can be very different!

Hence you need to get to know the local churches - who's attending; what have they got going and how they welcome new people?

* The churches are becoming more open in their outlook and more aware of social issues. You are likely to get a more understanding response than in days gone by.

* The churches are working more together and are less preoccupied by issues of denominationalism. They are likely to welcome people of all denominations and of none.

* The church is faced with many issues today - falling numbers; shortage of money, hence the clergy and leaders are weighed down with many responsibilities. Ask church leaders to put you in touch with one or two people from their congregation whom they think would be able to assist, rather than expecting the minister or priest to be the main point of contact.

* On the whole, the clergy have had little experience of dealing with people who have disabilities. They will need educating as much as their congregation. Ministers who ask for help are likely to prove more useful allies. The most frequent concern is difficulty in communicating with people who have a disability.

Figure:
What people with learning disabilities could offer churches

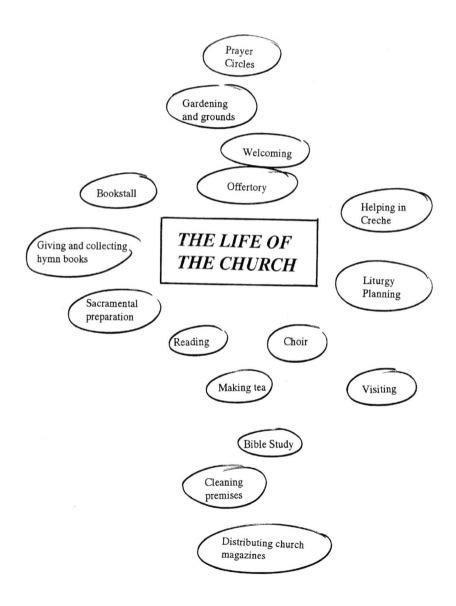

* Churches need people to get the job done. Stress the contribution which people with learning disabilities have made, and could make to the life of congregations (see Figure opposite).

* Be patient! The church, as with other human agencies, is slow to accept change. Among older people especially, the feeling may persist that people with disabilities are better cared for in institutions. Their attitudes can be patronising (see p. 21).

* A four point case can be made for churches involving themselves with people who are disabled:

   ♣ God's concern for the wellbeing of everyone;
   ♣ His command to love one another;
   ♣ The examples from the ministry of Jesus;
   ♣ Faith is expressed in our works.

What Churches Have To Offer

Within our society, churches can offer children and adults with learning disabilities a wide range of opportunities as the Figure overleaf illustrates. Some of these activities are also offered by other community groups but the church has a particular role to play in meeting the spiritual needs of a person.

A primary outcome of linking people with churches, is that they become part of the social networks found in churches and that they may also develop particular friendships. One man found a shared interest in cricket with a member of his church and together they went to Saturday matches. People with learning disabilities have a dearth of friendships outside of the specialist services.

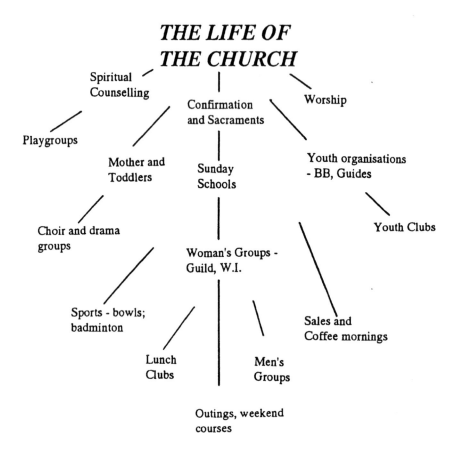

THE LIFE OF THE CHURCH

- Spiritual Counselling
- Playgroups
- Confirmation and Sacraments
- Worship
- Mother and Toddlers
- Sunday Schools
- Youth organisations - BB, Guides
- Choir and drama groups
- Woman's Groups - Guild, W.I.
- Youth Clubs
- Sports - bowls; badminton
- Sales and Coffee mornings
- Lunch Clubs
- Men's Groups
- Outings, weekend courses

Approaching Churches

* Find out what you can about a local church; ask around colleagues, neighbours etc. Look out for church notices in the local papers.

* Take time to visit the churches in the neighbourhood. For example one support worker took a resident from the group home to five local churches so that he could decide the one which he

preferred. He opted for one that was most welcoming rather than the denomination into which he had been baptised.

* Among the participants in the workshop, there was agreement that a person's denominational history should not preclude them from joining other churches.

* Prior contact with the minister or other leaders can be justified; especially if it helps to identify certain members of the church who might 'befriend' the new members. A word of warning; the people nominated tend to be professionals, such as primary school teachers! You may need to stress that personality is more important.

* Some churches have appointed pastoral care workers. They may be an excellent point of contact as they may have built up a network of 'supporters'.

* In talking to churches, stress the active involvement which people could make. One young man preferred going to the Salvation Army because they involved him in serving teas!

* Start small. It is better to introduce people to a church one at a time rather as a group. The risk with groups is that they are left to themselves and church members may feel more intimidated. When one person has settled in to the church, they may invite another person from their residence along. This strategy model has worked well.

* Encourage open communication. If the church encounters a problem they should be open about it with the person; stating their true feelings. Churches may also need the support and help of named people in a service whom they can approach to discuss problems. An example was given of how staff in a residence had

helped when a lady resident had become obsessed with the minister.

* People with a learning disability are the best educators of the public. Their active involvement in congregations has won people over. They also have a right to be there and their presence can enrich the church.

* That said, there are churches who will be unwelcoming. Very often the person with a learning disability can sense this. One bad experience should not put off making approaches to other churches.

* Talks to church groups, or as part of a church service, can stimulate interest and also be considered as part of a wider education of communities about the unmet needs of this client group. These might help set the scene for a later approach with an individual in mind.

* In sum, seek out churches which are open, flexible, whose members look out for one another and above all, who have a sense of humour!

Common Blocks

The speakers and participants in the workshop identified a number of common blocks. These are identified in this section and although no immediate solutions were forthcoming some ideas are presented.

Attitudes of care workers

Many of the younger care workers in services have little or no experience of attending churches. They may be reluctant to assist persons in going to church services which would not be the case in taking them to pubs or discos!

Care workers may be antagonistic to their clients getting involved with churches; fearing indoctrination etc.

Other workers may be embarrassed and unsure of issues to do with spirituality and tend to avoid any discussion of them.

These issues and others like them need to be discussed within services. Has the service a policy on religious observance and the expectations which they have of their staff? How can staff support clients without imposing their beliefs?

Special church events

Organising special 'religious' events for people with learning disabilities has its attractions, primarily the opportunity to devise services and activities which are adapted to their needs. For example:

* The Church of Scotland has recently published a confirmation programme for 'people with moderate learning difficulties' which can be used as a one-to-one course or with a small group of people with disabilities.

* The SPRED programme, operating in the Archdiocese of Glasgow and the Dioceses of Motherwell and Paisley as well as elsewhere in Britain, Ireland, U.S.A. and Australia, uses innovative forms of liturgy so that people regardless of the degree of their disability can be involved.

* *Faith and Light* is an inter-denominational organisation which operates in local parishes. The aim is to bring together people with disabilities and those without, to share their faith in celebrations and social activities.

The main criticism of special church events is that some of them tend to segregate and marginalise people with disabilities from the mainstream activities of the church. Some people with disabilities will avoid them for this reason. However, such criticism is tempered if participation is encouraged from non-handicapped people; or the special events can become a preparation for participation in the life of the church and the benefits they offer start to be incorporated into the mainstream worship of the church which is beginning to happen, such as with SPRED.

Patronising attitudes encountered in churches

Although not peculiar to churches, there may be a greater propensity for members to hold patronising attitudes in the belief that they are showing Christian charity but in reality masking their own insecurities.

Among the precautions which services can take are, avoid taking people in groups; importance of age-appropriate dress; redirecting questions to the people with disabilities so that they speak for themselves and getting them involved in making an active contribution to church life (see earlier).

Although opportunities may not arise easily, some form of 'disability awareness' training would prove useful and could be offered. In extreme circumstances, it might be better to try another church!

Meeting client's spiritual needs

This topic has received little attention in services and in churches. At a minimum we need to be aware of each individual's needs and provide opportunities for private devotions; for sharing in fellowship with other believers and for participation in the sacraments.

Moral issues; a person's needs for forgiveness and grief for the loss of a loved one all bring a spiritual dimension to our care. The need for trusted relationships and shared experiences was stressed by workshop participants so that people can vocalise their feelings and fears.

The Theology of Disability

Workshop participants noted that many churches had yet to work out a theology of disability that values the person as they are. Old notions of sinfulness and suffering often feature in thinking about disability. Some consolation can be had in the notion that concrete actions at parish level are more significant than debates in synods and assemblies. And these experiences will help to mould a theology which emphasises full participation and equality for people with disabilities.

Useful Books and Resources

Mental Handicap: Challenge to the Church edited by Brian Kelly & Patrick McGinley.

Going Places with Volunteers by Brian Kelly.

Both of these publications are available from: *Lisieux Hall Publications, Brothers of Charity, Whittle-le-Wood, Chorley, Lancs. PR6 7DX.*

Walk in God's Ways: A confirmation programme for candidates with moderate learning difficulties. Available from: Curriculum Development Unit of the Board of Parish Education, Church of Scotland, 121 George Street, Edinburgh EH2 4YN

Church Resource Pack for Community Involvement. Available from the Shaftesbury Society, 18-20 Kingston Road, London SW19 1JZ

Who's that sitting in my pew: Mentally Handicapped People in the Church by Faith Bowers. Published by Triangle/SPCK Books, Holy Trinity Church, Marylebone Road, London NW1 4DU.

Facilitating the role of local churches in the support networks of people with mental handicap. Final report by James Hogg. Available from: Mental Health Foundation, 37, Mortimer Street, London W1N 7RJ

Contact Addresses

SPRED, c/o St. Thomas' Primary School, 8 Smithycroft Road, Glasgow G33 2QJ

Faith and Light, c/o Ceili Horsborough, 3 Forestfield, Kelso, Scottish Borders

Workshop Participants

Catherine Appleton, Barnardo's, Glasgow
Margaret Gruber, Archdiocese of Glasgow Social Services
Monique Carr, Archdiocese of Glasgow Social Services
Sheila Middleton, Key Housing, Helensburgh
Bobby Jones, Key Housing, Govan, Glasgow
Jennifer Montgomery, Pastoral Worker, Newtown Mearns
Anita Campbell, Key Housing, Lanark
Barbara King, Key Housing, Lanark,
Ann Marshall, Key Housing, Milngavie
Pauline Crombie, Bonnington Centre, Edinburgh
Ian Turnbull, Churches Liaison Officer,
Tayside Regional Council

SECTION 3
TIPS AND TECHNIQUES

Educating communities about learning disability can take many forms and hence requires many diverse talents and skills from the people undertaking this work. Juggling is too small a word for it!

... ANYTHING YOU CAN DO... I CAN DO BETTER ! ...

In this section, the advice of experienced 'educators' is summarised along with the suggestions and ideas of network members who attended the training workshops on these topics.

The topics which proved of particular interest were:

☐ Working with People who have Learning
Disabilities on Educating Communities

☐ Finding Volunteers

☐ Involving People with Profound Disabilities in
Community Life

☐ Using Video

☐ Surveying Community Attitudes

☐ Evaluating the Impact of Community Initiatives

A common reaction from all workshop participants was that these skills can really only be mastered through putting them into practice rather than through reading and discussion. Being willing to risk failure is probably the first attribute of a budding educator of communities!

WORKING WITH PEOPLE WHO HAVE LEARNING DISABILITIES

People with learning disabilities are their own best ambassadors. But the very nature of their disability makes it hard for them to play an active part as educators of others; in particular the problems many experience in communicating and in understanding.

However, as with many other aspects of their lives, the risk is that professionals under-estimate their capacity to learn and to adapt to new demands. Hence this section is written primarily for professional workers as an encouragement to them to involve people with learning disabilities in the planning and carrying out of educational initiatives. An example is given of how the staff and users of one Scottish Resource Centre worked together on educating their local community.

Invariably it is the more able and verbally proficient people with learning disabilities who can become most active in educating communities. This obvious reality should not preclude efforts to widen the involvement to other more severely handicapped persons, perhaps assisted by people who know them well enough to speak on their behalf.

Promoting Self-Advocacy

A priority is to provide opportunities for people to advocate for themselves. In recent years, services have become more aware of the need to do this and of the range of ways by which self-advocacy can be encouraged; such as in client reviews, regular house meetings for people sharing the same accommodation and by having elected committees to advise service managers. All these experiences provide valuable learning opportunities for people with learning disabilities and are a vital prelude to engaging with them on the specific task of planning community education initiatives.

We asked a group of some 30 self-advocates to share their experiences of what had helped them to speak up for themselves. Here are the answers they gave arranged around three key themes of gaining confidence; getting help and speaking up for yourself.

Gaining Confidence

* Being an independent person - able and willing to stick up for yourself

* Training courses will develop confidence; help to get to know each other and become closer

* Join a Committee

* You get confidence from experience and practice

* Attend training course on how to be assertive

* Confidence comes from shopping for oneself

* Getting a job helps you speak up

* Know your rights - use an adviser

* Support each other within groups

Getting Help

* Get help from staff if needed

* Smaller meetings give people practice

* Draw pictures as well as writing and speaking

* Important for staff to encourage people to speak up

* Easier if you are with people you know

* Take your time no matter how long it takes

Speaking up

* Good clear voice; speak slowly and clearly

* If you have not heard a person ask them to repeat

* Give examples to explain what you mean

* Use words that people can understand

* Put your hand up to show people you have something to say

* Help people who cannot speak up to get their message across

* Keep on saying what you want until people listen

* Ask questions

* Practice with a tape-recorder

* Say what you think or feel

* Chairperson checks with members of the group if they want to say anything

* Take minutes, notes of the meeting and send them round to everyone to help them remember what was agreed.

The books referenced at the end of this section give further suggestions to both participants and facilitators of self-advocacy groups (see p. 155).

Priorities in Educating Communities

Working with self-advocates on educating communities invariably raises a number of key issues; some of which need to be handled sensitively. Among the ones which commonly occur in our experience are:

Labels The terminology of disability is of primary concern to many self-advocates who hold strong views as to what is acceptable. A consensus can be hard to achieve but discussions on this topic are often invaluable and this issue provides a useful way into many of the others which follow.

What Does it mean to be Disabled? Tackling issues of difference between people labelled 'disabled' and those who are not, can also be fraught with tensions. Among the more difficult to handle in groups are people's denial of their disabilities and a desire to exclude people with more severe disabilities as they feel stigmatised by association with them.

What Changes do we want to bring about? Most self-advocates have no difficulty with providing a 'wish' list; and quite an imaginative one at that but then who's to say what is realistic or not. Getting agreement on some key changes is usually easy enough although some people are preoccupied with their own concerns and find it hard to see another's point of view.

What Messages do we want to get across? Here too, advocates have a wealth of experiences to draw upon and as we outlined on p. 39, they can quickly come up with a list of what they would tell people if they had the chance!

How to get the Message Across Advocates will come up with plenty of ideas here too. In my experience they are willing and eager to meet with people although they may need help to plan the details of this. One drawback for them is that they may be unaware of the range of methods available for communicating information and they need to experience them in action before they can make an informed choice.

Prevention Perhaps the most sensitive issue of all, is promoting ways of preventing the birth of people with learning disabilities. The implicit message can be that people with disabilities are a burden to parents and society and should be eliminated. Some disability activists are now strong anti-abortionists arguing that this legitimises other discriminatory practices.

This debate raises so many moral and ethical issues that no quick agreement will be found on the rights and wrongs of prevention. However this argument needs to be separated from a decision about making information and knowledge available so that people can make their own informed choices.

Involvement as Educators

Advocates have a vital role to play as front-line educators. This can take many forms, including giving talks, answering questions as a panel member, putting together a photographic display and making a video programme.

Practice   As with any other person, people should be chosen for these roles on their aptitudes and interests. Even then, most will benefit from the chance to practice. This is especially so when people are giving a presentation or answering questions. They may need help with working out what they want to say; how to put this into the right words and the way they put the message across. It may be necessary to provide the the person with 'prompts' so that they remember all the points. Slides or overhead transparencies are good for doing this.

Honest feedback from a group of peers is a spur to improvement. This should highlight what was good as well as what needs improving.

Here's the advice of self-advocates with experience of speaking in public:

"Always have two 'trainers' with a group - support for each other if challenged; the other person can take over if one gets stuck.

"Keep your presentation entertaining - use jokes, songs, video clips".

"Tell people about your own experiences - they will listen!"

"Be proud of yourself - I am who I am"

"Avoid negative images - tragic but brave; and too many medical images"

Focus on Abilities As we noted earlier (p. 25) meeting people with learning disabilities is one of the most effective ways of changing people's perceptions. Such meetings need to promote people's abilities rather than their disabilities.

Meetings do not need to be contrived; opportunities can occur incidentally. For example, at an Arts and Craft Exhibition, the refreshments can be served by people with learning disabilities; demonstrations of craft work are performed by them and they can act as guides to the displays. Similar exhibitions can be mounted to show the employment potential of people with disabilities.

As with anyone else, people will perform their roles better if they have a chance to practice and are given feedback about how they could do it better.

Evaluating Impact Finally, people with disabilities are key informants when it comes to reviewing the impact of the educational initiatives in which they have been involved (see p. 223). Their experiences can be contrasted with those reported beforehand and any benefits noted. Likewise any necessary changes can be documented for future reference.

An Example of Working Together

Kemback Street Adult Resource Centre provides day services to around 80 men and women with learning disabilities in Dundee. The Centre's aim is to promote social independence and normal patterns of living. A considerable amount of staff time is concentrated on the personal development of centre-users; particularly their social skills. But often this work is undermined by the reactions of the local community to people attending the Centre and also sometimes by the client's own behaviour. Behaviours which others found embarrassing or inappropriate was at best tolerated and at worst negatively reinforced in many social situations.

The idea emerged of undertaking a neighbourhood survey; the beginning of a dialogue with the local community around Kemback Centre and through involving clients at all stages in the project, to challenge many of the prejudices against people with learning disabilities.

The aims of the survey defined by those taking part in it, were:

* to collect information on the general public's attitudes towards people with learning disabilities;
* to open the Centre to the wider public;
* to evaluate the community presence of people from the centre;
* to act as an educational initiative with the local community
* to survey local perceptions of the Centre.

Our objectives included:

* to have fun;
* to learn new skills, especially how to do surveys;
* to improve the service provided by the Centre;
* for staff and clients to work together with real participation by clients;
* to help people's self-confidence;
* to adapt and apply research methods to local community surveys.

A steering group for the project was set up, consisting of four clients, three day centre staff and the Social Work Department's Development Officer (Learning Disabilities). An Assistant Principal Officer from the Department's Research and Information Technology Section also joined the group to give 'expert' advice. This group met regularly over a period of about 18 months to discuss, plan and undertake the survey. This meant that everyone involved was able to learn and practice new skills. The group meetings evolved to become an important part of the participative process.

Prior to piloting the questionnaires all members of the group participated in a training course organised by the Department's Training Section concentrating on assertiveness skills and taking part in role play exercises of typical situations we might encounter. Two members of the group also attended a one day course organised by the Educating Communities Network on conducting local surveys.

Two questionnaires were drawn up by the group to survey the neighbours and shops around Kemback Street Centre in the summer of 1992. People from the Centre, both staff and clients, knocked on the doors of the houses close to the centre. Around 250 households were targeted. We told them what the questionnaire was for and left it with them to complete. Some questionnaires were collected a couple of days later and some were posted back to us in the prepaid envelopes we left.

Two of the group went around the shops on Albert Street, the main shopping area close to the centre, We handed the questionnaire to as many people as were working in the shops or however many people were willing to fill them in. In some of the shops therefore we left multiple copies of the questionnaire. The shops included a large supermarket, several banks, bakeries, hairdressers, second-hand furniture shops, charity shops, bookmakers, chemists, butchers, cafes, takeaway foods and pet shops. Again questionnaires were collected a few days later or were returned in the envelopes left.

The results of the survey were analysed on a personal computer at Social Work Headquarters and again, centre users were involved in inputting the data, and designing the charts which illustrated the results.

Service users have given presentations about the survey to various groups.

The group planned and mounted an Open Day to which local people were invited.

The Future

Ultimately the principle beneficiaries of a better educated community are the people with disabilities. It is doubly ironic then that the attitude of doing things for them still pervades so much of our thinking in services and among families. Often the excuse adopted is that our 'clients' aren't able for this work and it would put too much pressure on them. Perhaps it is these attitudes more than other which gets in the way of people becoming fuller members of the community. Promoting self-advocacy and joint-working is therefore an essential starting point.

Further Reading

Learning about Self-Advocacy. Available from: *Values into Action, 5 Kentings, Comberton, Cambs. CB3 7DT*

Whose Lifestyle? A package to enable people with learning disabilities to speak from themselves, by Hilary Brown.
Available from: *Pavilion Publishing, Freepost (BR 458), 8 St. George's Place, Brighton, East Sussex BN1 4ZZ*

Sticking Up for Yourself: Self-advocacy and people with learning disabilities by K. Simons and J. Carter

Quality in Action: A resource pack for improving services for people with learning difficulties.

Both of these packs are available from: *Norah Fry Research Centre, 32, Tyndall's Park Road, Bristol BS8 1PY*

Better Meetings: A Handbook for individuals, groups and trainers
Open University Community Education, Milton Keynes

Working Together: Open University Course P555(M)

Both packs are available from: *Learning Materials Sales Office, Open University, P.O.Box 188, Milton Keynes MK7 6DH*

FINDING AND SUPPORTING VOLUNTEERS

Volunteering has never enjoyed a higher profile than at present. The work of volunteers among individuals with learning disabilities makes a valuable contribution to their quality of life. With more people now living in community settings there is greater scope and need for ordinary men and women to volunteer their help.

Recent surveys reveal that people in Scotland are more involved in voluntary work than other parts of the U.K. Statistics cited by Volunteer Development Scotland (1990-1991) show that 51% of adult Scots, undertake some form of voluntary activity. Of this group, 70% are married and a slightly larger proportion of women to men form the volunteer workforce. A wide age range is represented, although the majority of volunteers fall within the 25-54 year age group.

No statistics are available about the deployment of volunteers with people who have learning disabilities but it is likely to be a considerable number throughout the country. Past research also suggests that as many as one in four neighbours in a housing estate are willing to be of 'help', e.g. inviting a resident of the home to visit their house (see p. 22). However a common complaint made by neighbours was that they had not been asked to help and they did not like to offer in case they were thought of as nosey! The issue is not so much that the public is unwilling to volunteer their help; rather professional services have not found ways of recruiting and supporting volunteers.

Hence this section of the book provides basic guidelines for service personnel and interested others who may be thinking about, or actively planning projects which involve the participation of volunteers in the lives of people with learning disabilities.

Advantages for People with learning disabilities

Involving volunteers in the lives of people with learning disabilities has many advantages:

• *Company* - both for the individual with learning disabilities and for the volunteer, as they share time together in various situations.

• *Opportunities for Experience* - are provided, which enable both parties to learn from each other.

• *A Sense of Self-Identity* - usually results from feedback which individuals offer to one another, as a relationship develops.

• *Increased Self-Esteem* - for both the volunteer and the person with a learning disability, as their individual role within the relationship becomes clearer and is reinforced.

• *Security and Intimacy* - may develop over time and provides a sense of closeness and trust which enriches friendships.

• *Practical Help* - can be provided in small ways, which serve to increase the individual's quality of life.

• *Greater Community Integration* - as individuals with learning disabilities have greater opportunities to widen their involvement within the local community.

There are also many issues to be considered when trying to find and support volunteers; namely effective methods of recruitment, their selection and screening; payment and insurance; training and support.

These issues and others were tackled in a one-day workshop organised by the Educating Communities Network. Three speakers shared their experiences of recruiting and supporting volunteers in a range of projects and these were augmented through discussed among the workshop participants who came from various parts of Scotland. Their conclusions and recommendations are presented here.

Our guests were:

✿ Kim Lyster, Director of Community Relations, British
        Columbia Association for Community Living, Vancouver

✿ Fiona Hardie, Volunteer Development Scotland Project,
        Strathmartine Hospital, Dundee

✿ Rachel Ball, Quarrier's Home Life Project, Drumchapel.

The Canadian Experience - Kim Lyster

The British Columbia Association for Community Living aims to provide new styles of services for people with learning disabilities. In urban areas and rural towns they have used volunteers to widen people's network of friends.

Adults with learning disabilities are encouraged to join local advocacy groups where they express their own wishes regarding leisure interests and any other activities which they would like to become involved in.

The volunteer scheme relies heavily on the service organisers using all their own contacts within the local community, whether work related or personal. Good 'sales and marketing' skills are needed to entice ordinary people into the schemes. Successful ventures include part-time employment, shared sporting activities, church related activities, parties and socials.

Kim believes that people with learning disabilities should be given the same freedom as others to become involved in new relationships, despite the inevitable risks. As friendships mature, the organiser should withdraw and let the folk get on with it! Kim's philosophy is that "Community Building" can only be achieved when individuals are encouraged to give of themselves in reciprocal relationships.

She sees the process as an art rather than a science, and the relationship is as important as the ultimate goal of planned activities.

Further Information: Kim Lyster, British Association for Community Living, 300-30 East 6th Ave., Vancouver BC V5T 4P4, Canada.

Volunteers in a Mental Handicap Hospitals - Fiona Hardie.

Fiona Hardie was the first co-ordinator of an ongoing project in Strathmartine Hospital, Dundee; funded by a Scottish Home and Health grant to Volunteer Development Scotland. The project, which has now been running for three years, aims to improve the quality of life of adults with learning disabilities (especially those with severe and profound disabilities) who have been living in long-stay hospital wards for much of their lives.

The recruitment of volunteers is a highly competitive market, hence Fiona uses various means of recruitment - press releases to local papers, articles for special journals, posters circulated round libraries, local shops, Post Offices, etc. She also gives talks to various community groups about the project. Of all these methods, a leaflet about the project has proved the most effective.

Since the work is hospital based, volunteers work alongside paid staff in pairs or small groups, although they may also take people on outings. Most of the staff have known the adults for many years and thus are able to provide valuable insight into possible ways to build a successful friendship with the individuals.

The scheme has a code of practice for volunteers to follow but they are also encouraged to make decisions regarding activities with their new adult friends through joint discussion. Fiona emphasises that the specific activities engaged in are less important than the individual attention which the residents receive.

The Strathmartine project offers training in the form of various workshops to their volunteers on topics they have requested and also provides regular support for them.

Further Information: Volunteer Project, Strathmartine Hospital, Dundee,

Quarriers Friendship Scheme - Rachel Ball

The Quarriers Home Life Project is working in seven 'priority treatment' areas in and around Glasgow. They are aiming to develop a number of community initiatives of which the Friendship Scheme is one. This aims to match people of varying abilities with volunteers from their local communities.

The focus of the friendship is on shared leisure activities and Rachel's role is to provide support and monitoring for both parties involved.

Initially, Rachel herself invites the adult with learning disabilities to go out with her informally, e.g. for coffee, in order to assess how the individual engages with a stranger, in a social situation. She also gets to know the key people in the adult's life i.e. carers, family, day-centre staff.

Volunteers are invited to attend an induction programme, which involves looking at their own attitudes, barriers and anxieties about learning disabilities. The group also focuses on the development of social skills necessary to make and maintain friendships.

As with the other projects, Rachel's involvement, as co-ordinator, is gradually phased out as the friendship develops, leaving both parties the freedom to make decisions, on an equal basis, without feeling under "supervision".

Further Information: Quarrier's Home Life Project, 31 Kendoon Ave., Drumchapel, Glasgow.

Using the experiences of these three projects plus those of the workshop participants, recommendations for finding and supporting volunteer helpers were drawn up. These now follow.

Roles and Tasks for Volunteers

The more common roles which British volunteers are presently fulfilling, are:

○ Volunteers offering general help to paid staff in certain work situations, e.g. hospitals, or as bus drivers etc.

○ Volunteers offering a different experience for people with learning disabilities, by accompanying them to events and places, which they might otherwise never go to. Volunteers are often well equipped with local knowledge about events and places to attend.

○ Linking volunteers and adults together who have similar leisure interests which they share on a regular basis. Through these people with learning disabilities can be introduced to clubs etc.

○ Volunteers involved in respite care schemes can provide breaks for both the parents/carers and the adults themselves.

○ Work experience or supported employment schemes often depend on volunteers from the workforce to act as befrienders or as a job 'coach'.

○ There is also scope for volunteers to become involved in 'behind the scene' tasks, e.g. office work, planning events and the production of resource packs.

A common conclusion was that:

The relationships which develop are more important than the particular tasks which volunteers undertake. However shared activities are good spring-boards for making acquaintances from which friendships can grow.

From this, the workshop participants went on to review some of the other roles which volunteer helpers might fulfil.

New Roles for Volunteers

■ To look at the quality of the services being offered, and encourage greater advocacy by the service-user or to act as an advocate on their behalf.

■ To provide more imaginative respite schemes to children and adults with learning disabilities that gives them a positive experience while enabling their families to have a break in caring.

■ To counteract, through befriending schemes, the loneliness and inactivity which can beset people with learning disabilities living alone.

■ To aid community awareness of learning disabilities and to enhance the integration of adults with a disability into the community, thus breaking down barriers in neighbourhoods, leisure clubs etc.

■ To use experienced volunteers as recruiters and trainers of others; thereby encouraging ripple effects within communities and the building of circles of friendships.

But for these developments to happen:

Services need to be more precise in identifying the specific needs of their users and more imaginative as to how they could be met.

Recruiting Volunteers

♦ The recruitment of volunteers needs to be ongoing for just as there is a turn-over with paid staff so too volunteers will leave.

♦ Use your own personal contacts in the locality to spread the news of your work. Encourage your co-workers to do the same.

♦ Prepare a leaflet describing your need for voluntary help. Use illustrations - keep the wording simple and direct. Provide contact address and phone number.

♦ Use publicity, i.e. leaflets, posters in public places, e.g. library, G.Ps. waiting room, churches, volunteer bureau, coffee shops.

♦ Send press release to local newspaper or radio stations describing the scheme. Follow these with a phone call.

♦ If you are having social events for existing volunteers, get them to bring along a friend.

♦ Word of mouth can be particularly effective in small communities.

♦ Go to organisations whose members can benefit from getting involved in volunteering, e.g. Boy's Brigade, Girl's Brigade, Duke of Edinburgh Award schemes etc.

♦ Approach the officers of clubs and organisations. Ask them to recommend possible people whom you might approach.

♦ Likewise search out the people in the community who are most knowledgeable about what's happening locally. Get their advice as to how people with learning disabilities might fit in and their recommendations for people you could approach.

♦ Give talks to local groups - Woman's Guilds, Rotary etc. - bring along a volunteer to share their experience or show video of volunteers at 'work' and talking about it.

Two other points are worth noting -

♦ Use people with learning disabilities as co-recruiters.

♦ In all your publicity, spell out the benefits to having volunteers in your work and what people are likely to get out of it.   Use quotes from existing volunteers.

Relying on only one means of recruitment is not enough.   Use a variety of means, e.g. leaflets, adverts, press releases, word of mouth etc.

Selection and Safeguards

A variety of selection procedures may be implemented by an organisation, these can include;

♦ Having a general meeting at first (without commitment) but inviting interested people to return for further meeting(s).

♦ Application forms can be completed by each prospective volunteer, to provide essential demographic information.   The volunteer can also be asked to give names of two people to give character references.

♦ Interviews are best kept informal and tend to be more effective when the volunteer is interviewed by two staff members.

♦ It is always good procedure to inform prospective volunteers of any decision regarding acceptance or rejection, in writing, giving reasons for not accepting someone who has applied to be a volunteer.

♦ Some organisations prefer to outline their expectations of volunteers, in an informal "contract" which both parties sign.

♦ People with learning disabilities and the volunteers should be allowed to have a say in the choice of "friend" to whom they are linked .

In order to protect themselves and people with learning disabilities, some organisations prefer to employ certain safeguards, such as police checks. Such procedures are not always available to small agencies; they can take several months to complete and can be off-putting for volunteers. Others will argue that excessive checks are not necessary. This issue remains a controversial topic and inevitably organisations will adopt their own policies.

Confidentiality It is also important to work out just how much information should be given to each partner in the "friendship" about the other, and also to the carers of the adults involved. This will likely vary according to the type and frequency of contacts between volunteers and people with learning disabilities.

Training, Support and Recognition

Some form of preparation is needed for volunteers but there are reservations about providing 'formal' training sessions:

■ Formal training can imply that the volunteer does not have anything to offer as they are, and that we must shape them in the image of the 'professionals' before they can be of use.

■ It reinforces stereotypes of these people as different who need special treatments.

■ It may create a dependency on professionals and establish their 'power' over the volunteers.

■ The best learning takes place in real-life settings rather than lecture rooms.

However, volunteers may request information about certain topics and issues. It is best to take your lead from them and their perceived needs rather than organising pre-planned courses. 'Training' can also be done on a one-to-one basis as well as in groups. People with learning disabilities can be invited to participate.

Also some people may have built up myths about disabled people, so some 'values based' training may be of more relevance than knowledge-based training.

Practical skills training could include (as appropriate to the needs of the people with whom they are linked): emergency first aid, lifting and handling, coping with epilepsy and communication aids.

Support

Volunteers should have a name and phone number of a person they can contact, e.g. the organiser of the project. The volunteers should be confident in being able to approach him or her.

Support can also take the form of a "circle of friends", comprising volunteers, staff and people with learning disabilities. Social evenings and reviews provide opportunities to reflect on experiences.

In some situations, it may be feasible to introduce a volunteer to other people in the life of their "friend", e.g. parent, key-worker who can also provide ongoing support.

For volunteers working with people whose communication skills are poor, it is especially necessary to give them regular feedback about what their involvement means to the person.

Recognition

Although it is important to recognise the work of volunteers this should never be done in a patronising or cliche fashion. Always provide an opportunity for volunteers to express their own opinions about how the relationship is working, and, where possible, offer advice if felt necessary.

Letters and cards all help to make volunteers feel part of the team. Newsletters may be valuable in larger schemes.

Invitations to socials and special events help to mark their contribution.

Service Practices

The involvement of volunteers may not pose any difficulties to the existing service, but sometimes conflicts may arise.

☐ Existing paid staff may feel threatened by the presence of new faces in the workplace, therefore it is important to give detailed descriptions of the precise role which the volunteer is permitted to undertake. It should be made clear that volunteers are not there to do the work of paid staff.

☐ Each organisation will have their own insurance policies to negotiate and there is no one fast rule regarding the issue of liability. Check with the service administration. Volunteer Development Scotland has a special policy which projects can avail of.

☐ Volunteers using their cars whilst engaged on voluntary work should get clearance for their motor insurers.

☐ All the expenses incurred by volunteers should be reimbursed regardless of their own financial status. Hence some budgetary provision must be made for this work.

☐ Volunteers should not have to cover the expenses of people with learning disabilities. Families or staff in residences should be briefed about this.

☐ Guidelines may be helpful in outlining how volunteers should react, in the event of a conflict arising between the adult and their carer over some issue relating to a planned activity.

Terminology

Clear guidance needs to be given to volunteers as to the preferred terms for people with learning disabilities.

Equally some people prefer not to use the word "volunteering", as it implies a "power" relationship, with only one party giving of themselves, while the other does the receiving. Other alternatives include, "friendship", "befriending" and "community helpers".

Further Information on Volunteering

Volunteer Development Scotland; 80, Murray Place, Stirling FK8 2BX

Volunteer Development Scotland is the national resource and development agency in Scotland, on volunteers and volunteer work. It aims to promote and support volunteering in Scotland and encourages the implementation of policies regarding volunteers, within organisations. Among the services they offer are: Information and Advice Support, Consultancy; Publications; Research; Conferences and Seminars.
Their publications include:
Recruiting, selecting and vetting volunteers
From good intent to effective action: Volunteer co-ordinators
describe their work.
Training and volunteering
Directory of Volunteer Bureaux in Scotland

The Volunteer Centre, U.K., Carriage Row, 183, Eversholt Street, London NW11 1BU.

The Volunteer Centre, U.K. is a registered charity, which aims to promote volunteering among varied groups in the community. It encourages good practice in the involvement of volunteers, whether in the statutory or private sectors. The Centre acts as a resource agency for policy makers, managers and volunteer organisers. An information catalogue listing resource materials, which include Volunteer Handbooks, Good Practice Guides and many other publications of interest are available. Their publications include:

Working it Out : Some Guidelines for Project Organisers This booklet offers concise advice to organisers of volunteer projects, helping to answer questions such as : "Why do I want volunteers, rather than paid staff?" "How do I manage and support volunteers?"

Support Advice on how volunteers should be supported

All expenses paid A guide on reimbursement of expenses.

Volunteers First Personnel responsibilities of people who manage volunteers

Involving Volunteers with Mentally Handicapped People

Volunteers and Community Care (1990) This booklet discusses volunteering with reference to government policy and offers practical advice on how to draw up local plans for the involvement of volunteers with service users, to the benefit of both.

Further Reading

Let's Make Friends *Jodie Walsh, London, Souvenir Press (1985)*
Provides detailed information about the use of volunteers within services with particular emphasis on recruiting families to provide short-term breaks and 'befrienders' for adults with severe learning disabilities.

Going places with volunteers - creating an enabling community environment*Brian Kelly, Chorley, Lisieux Hall Publications (1991).*
Describes the setting up of a volunteer scheme within a service for adult persons with learning disabilities. Highly recommended. Available from: Lisieux Hall Publications, Whittle-le-Woods, Chorley, Lancs. PR6 7DX

Good practice guide for voluntary service co-ordinators in NHS
Available from: Advance, Brixton Enterprise Centre, 444 Brixton Road, London SW9 8EJ

The following books describe primarily the friendship needs of people with learning disabilities and how services might respond.

From Acquaintance to Friendship:
Hugh Firth and Mark Rapley,
Kidderminster, BIMH Publications, 1990

Innovations in Leisure and Recreation for people with a Mental Handicap
Roy McConkey and Patrick McGinley (editors), Chorley, Lisieux Hall Publications, 1990

Developing Friendships: Enabling People with Learning Difficulties to Make and Maintain Friends
Anne Richardson and Jane Ritchie, London, Policy Studies Institute, 1989

Circles of Friends: People with disabilities and their friends enrich the lives of one another.
London, V.I.A. Publications, Oxford House, Derbyshire Street, London E2 6HG

Training Packages

One-to-One: A guide to establishing and running local schemes through which people with learning difficulties can gain new friendships in their communities.
Contact: One-to-One, 404 Camden Road, London N7 0SJ

This resource pack aims to help local people set up schemes through people with learning disabilities can obtain new opportunities for friendship. The pack contains four guides; one for individuals setting up schemes; a second for salaried co-ordinators responsible for the day-to-day running of schemes and another gives information sheets, exercise materials, presentational aids and outline training schedules for friendship scheme volunteers. The final guide - 'Being a One-to-One Partner' - contains biographical information and materials relevant to the relationships enjoyed by friends. The pack was developed by the One-to-One organisation with grants from the Department of Health, King's Fund Centre and Marks and Spencer.

"Training Resource Packs 1 Volunteers in Community Care Services": 2 Volunteers with Extra Support Needs: 3 The Effective Management of Volunteers.
These packs contain everything needed to run 'in-house' training events, including information, background reading and training materials.
Available from: The Volunteer Centre U.K.

"Let's Befriend!"
A resource pack produced by the Befriending resources group is available through Volunteer Development Scotland.

Disability Awareness Training Pack
Contact: Learning Materials Service Office, Open University, P.O.Box 188, Milton Keynes MK7 6DH
This pack includes audio and video materials for use in disability awareness workshops organised for volunteers or other community groups.

Workshop Participants

Angela Coates, SSMH, Holiday Scheme
Pauline Crombie, Ranoch Centre, Edinburgh
Elizabeth Dyke, Development Officer, SSMH
Jill Gibson, FAIR, Edinburgh
Susan Govan, St Aidan's Centre, Gattonside
Marion Irvine, Action Group, Edinburgh
May MacLean, Toryglen Resource Centre, Glasgow
Jack Marshall, SSMH Holiday Scheme
Catherine Montgomery, Sheredeere Scheme, East Kilbride
Andrew Murray, ELCAP, East Lothian
Philip Russell, ELCAP, East Lothian
Jim Souter, Volunteer Helper, Ayr
Mark Sprott, Orbiston ATC, Belshill
Douglas Whittaker, Orbiston ATC, Bellshill

INVOLVING PEOPLE WITH PROFOUND DISABILITIES IN COMMUNITY ACTIVITIES

Profound disability is difficult to define precisely but in general, we take it to mean that the child or adult has problems with mobility, in communicating verbally and requires help with personal self-care including feeding and toileting. In addition the person may have sensory or physical disabilities, including epilepsy, as well as complex learning disabilities.

Although the majority of these people live - and have lived - with their families, the demands placed on their carers has left little energy for involvement with the community. Likewise the favoured alternative of placement in mental handicap hospitals has isolated them from the general public.

With increased community care initiatives, more energies are directed at supporting families; people with profound disabilities are attending day centres or living in community houses and some are being relocated from hospitals. However attitudinal research suggests that members of the public are especially reticent about meeting people with profound disabilities. Hence particular efforts may need to made in order to involve children and adults in the life of their local communities.

The workshop drew upon the experiences of participants in order to identify good practice in educating the community about profound disability and encouraging their involvement with people who have profound disabilities.

Our speakers were:

✿   Loretto Lambe, White Top Centre, Dundee and formerly Director of the Mencap sponsored project on Profound and Multiple Handicap, Manchester.

✿   Angie Wynn, Co-ordinator SSMH 'Lend-A-Hand' Scheme, Dunfermline.

✿   Haidee Summerwill, Carisbrooke Centre, Airdrie.

The content of the guide was further developed in four working groups which gave participants an opportunity to share their experiences and produce recommendations for action.

Coping with Disabilities

The starting point, as always, has to be with the person and their needs. However for children and adults with profound disabilities, their needs are likely to be manifold. Extra demands will be placed on the people who are involved with them either at home, in centres or clubs, or in community settings. In particular:

■ Dependency on wheel-chairs - 'helpers' need guidance on lifting; access to cars, taxis or specialised transport.

■ Require assistance with feeding - food may need to be liquidised; special cups are often required. Helpers need to be taught feeding techniques.

■ Little verbal communication - helpers have to learn the non-verbal signals which nearly all can use to communicate their likes, wants and moods. Hearing and vision problems may also be present.

■ Medication - most people with profound handicaps are taking medicines regularly.

■ Epilepsy - an increased incidence of epilepsy is found among people with profound disabilities. Helpers need to know how to cope with seizures.

■ Toileting - helpers may have to deal with double incontinence and invariably will need to assist people on and off the toilet.

(Further details about the characteristics of people with profound disabilities are contained in a survey carried out in England and Wales of nearly 2,000 children and adults with profound and multiple handicaps by Loretto Lambe and her colleagues. She is presently involved in a similar survey in Tayside, see p. 188).

Community Involvement

But these disabilities have not prevented people from joining in various community activities, albeit with support from staff in residences or centres, with the assistance sometimes of volunteer helpers or students in placements. Among the examples given by participants were -

○ Eating out - restaurants will liquidise food if asked. A phone call in advance can help to confirm this.

○ Pubs - people with disabilities seem to react better when there's plenty going on, e,g, music nights

○ Swimming - many pools have lifting equipment.

○ Shopping - especially local shops where shopkeepers can get to know the people.

○ Bowling - special equipment can be requested to help people bowl.

○ Cinemas - more are wheelchair accessible and special areas are provided.

○ Football matches - including all the extras; pre-match drink, half-time snack and post-match celebrations!

○ Fishing - fish farms provide all the equipment and facilities

○ Visits - museums, Butterfly farms, parks, leisure centres etc.

○ PHAB Clubs - these aim to integrate young people with physically handicaps and their non-handicapped age peers. Holidays and day trips are also organised in addition to weekly club nights.

At Carisbrooke Centre a weekly planner is made out of each person's community activities detailing who is going, what they will do and the transport they will use. These plans are summarised on a grid to ensure that each attender at the centre has their share of community outings and to ensure that each person experiences a variety of activities.

These outings are most successful when done in small groups of two or four people.

Common Difficulties

However a number of common difficulties were noted by participants, namely

☐ the lack of community facilities in more rural areas;

☐ problems in arranging suitable transport;

☐ difficulty in gaining access to public buildings. This can mean two able-bodied people accompanying a person in a wheelchair.

☐ people with profound disabilities can be resistant to change and unwilling to try new experiences;

☐ self-abusive behaviours; hyperactivity and loud vocalising are hard to manage in public settings.

☐ colleagues or managers in centres or residences who had little sympathy with the aims of involving the service users in community activities.

☐ finding activities that are appropriate to the person's age but which are meaningful to them.

Hence people with profound disabilities can join in community life but it requires special efforts and determination from their carers.

Involving People from the Community

Specially trained staff are NOT the only carers. Most families manage with little or no special training and as Angie Wynn described, ordinary people have successfully provided respite care in their homes for these children after short, focused training and with ongoing support.

However, the common experience was that people from the community appear to have particular fears about meeting a person with profound disabilities. In extreme form this has resulted in groups being asked to leave restaurants and pubs. However participants at the workshop noted a number of other problems.

● public reaction to people with behavioural problems or when a person have a seizure;

● teenagers and children vandalising a residence (throwing stones) and name calling;

● neighbours of residences giving no response when invited;

● easier to get volunteers to work with more able people and with children than it is for adult persons with profound disabilities.

Strategies for changing attitudes

Participants described various ways which had proved effective for them in shaping community attitudes:

* The example of care staff when they were with the person in community settings; in particular, talking to them, consulting with them about preferences; offering choices.

* Introducing the person to local shopkeepers etc. so that over time a relationship gets built up;

* Carers bringing the person to their home to meet family members, especially children;

* Social events such as dances or in pubs when people can meet in a relaxed atmosphere;

* Leisure schemes, play schemes and working as volunteers on special holidays had all proved useful in engaging teenagers with peers who were profoundly disabled.

* Videos of people with profound disabilities in activities with non-disabled peers. These can be shown prior to actual meetings taking place.

* Carers taking time to explain the particular needs of each individual and how they can be overcome; for instance if the person cannot hear.

* Young people on work experience or students on placement have influenced the attitudes of their families and peers.

What Can the Community Realistically Do?

As noted already, the demands of looking after a person with profound disabilities are many and it may be unrealistic to expect members of the public to cope with them. However workshop participants gave various examples of how people were assisting or could assist without placing unrealistic demands on them.

* Extra pair of hands when carers take people with profound disabilities on outings or on holidays.

* Linking with a resident who had no family contact to send birthday cards, postcards and occasional visits, outings etc.

* Looking after the person at home for a couple of hours to enable family carers to go out.

* Volunteer helper at day centre; working with person on shared interests

* Befriending a person; exchanging home visits.

* Respite carer, either by having the person to their own home or going to the family home to look after them. The Dunfermline scheme now has over fifty families providing respite care.

Recruiting Help

Among the most productive ways of recruiting helpers have been:

◆ Personal contacts: In the Lend-a-Hand Project most new carers come from the friends, neighbours and family of existing members.

◆ Posters: Simple clear posters can be produced at low cost and personal contacts used to have them displayed in local shops, libraries, health centres etc.

◆ Local Resources: Approaches can be made to local resources such as schools, Colleges, Community centres, Volunteer Bureau etc. when seeking helpers

◆ Community newsletters: Resident Associations, clubs and churches produce regular newsletters. Articles and notices in them have proved productive although it can take some time tracking down the editors!

Preparation and Training

Due to the particular needs of people with disabilities, community helpers must be offered some form of preparation and training. Otherwise they may feel unable to take on the responsibility and the person with the disabilities can be put at risk. The following topics were recommended, depending on the circumstances.

> * Lifting
> * Feeding
> * Communication
> * Coping with difficult behaviours
> * Particular health and hygiene procedures
> * How do you explain the handicap to others,
>   e.g. children.

How the training is done is just as important as the content. Participants recommended that:

● low key, informal approaches are preferable;

● opportunities to meet first in natural surroundings to get to know one another;

● the training builds up the confidence of 'natural' expertise of the trainee helpers;

● experienced carers - family members, staff or other volunteers - be fully involved in the training;

● the training is highly practical. Trainees should practice the techniques on each other. For example, being fed by another person; having a person brush your teeth!

• the information needs to be tailored to the individual(s) with whom the trainee is working.

• avoid having too many 'professionals' at training events. Community trainees can be inhibited.

A series of training packages have been published from the workshops undertaken as part of the Mencap Project described by Loretto Lambe. Further details are given later.

Service issues

At a practical level, service staff may need to check:

☐ Insurance cover. The service insurers should be informed.

☐ Car Insurance. If the community helpers will use their own car to transport the person with disabilities they will need to obtain an indemnity from their insurers.

☐ Police checks. These are required in respite care schemes.

☐ Clear written guidelines are available to helpers to cover particular situations.

☐ While respecting confidentiality, helpers may need a written summary of each person's particular needs and strengths with whom they are linked. This should include their medication; their interests; food and drink preferences; sensory strengths; physical competencies and usual means of communicating.

Ongoing Support

The interest and enthusiasm of community helpers can be sustained through:

♦ identified person with whom they are linked and who provides a constant point of contact.

♦ open door policy so that the helper feels free to make contact;

♦ regular support meetings and social events;

♦ friendly phone calls from link person to ensure that all is well;

♦ newsletter to keep people in touch with what is happening and to recognise their participation;

♦ enlisting their friends as helpers so that networks of mutual support develop;

♦ opportunities to attend review meetings;

♦ ongoing training sessions. These can be shared with others, such as family carers, service staff etc.

Conclusions

Christopher Nolan, the talented Irish writer with profound disabilities, describes in his autobiography a swimming expedition with his family; the efforts they expended to help him and the affect it has on him. He writes, "he glowed with pleasure as he skimmed along for he felt totally relaxed and safe in their hands and through their efforts he experienced the joys of the able-bodied" (p.104) That in a nutshell, is the challenge and task we face as we endeavour to involve people with profound disabilities in their local communities.

Contact Addresses

Loretto Lambe, White Top Centre, Dept. of Social Work, The University, Dundee

Angie Wynn, Lend-a-Hand Scheme, 57, Beath View, Dunfermline, Fife KY11 4UF

Carisbrooke Centre, Commonhead Avenue, Airdrie, Scotland

Further Reading and Resources

Learning for Life: A pack to support learning opportunities for adults who have profound intellectual and multiple physical disabilities, Further Education Unit/Mencap, 1994
Available from: Mencap Bookshop, 123 Golden Lane, London EC1Y 0RT

Denziloe, J. (1994).   *Fun & Games: Practical leisure ideas for people with profound disabilities*, London, Butterworth-Heinneman.

Hogg, J. & Cavet, J. (eds.) (1994). *Making leisure provision for people with profound learning and multiple disabilities*, London, Chapman & Hall.

Nolan, C. (1987).   *Under the Eye of the Clock,* London, Pan Books.

Workshop Participants

Emma Johns, The Action Group, Edinburgh
Kath Bruce, Orbiston Centre, Bellshill
Jean Ballantyne, McPherson Centre, Gourock
Katie Thomson, Strathlee Resource Centre, Kilmarnock
Scott Taylor, Inverurie, Aberdeenshire
Hazel Smylie, OT Department, Arrol Park Hospital, Ayr
Norma Hill, OT Department, Arrol Park Hospital, Ayr
John Abbotts, Bingham House, Edinburgh
Mary Laidlaw, Bingham House, Edinburgh
Fiona Hunter, Elcap, Haddington, East Lothian
Joanne Law, Elcap, Haddington, East Lothian
Trish Grierson, St Aidan's Centre, Gattonside, Borders
Martin McGarry, St Aidan's Centre, Gattonside, Borders
Yvonne Yale, Barnardo's Residential Services, Dundee
Ilene McCabe, Barnardo's Residential Services, Dundee
Kenny Martin, Barnardo's Residential Services, Dundee
Linda Ballantyne, Barnardo's Residential Services, Dundee
Cara Watts, Barnardo's Residential Services, Dundee
Tom McDonald, Key Housing, Thurso
Katherine Montgomery, Shared Care, Glasgow
Brenda Clark, Respite Carer, Blantyre
Linda Reid, Fred Martin Project, Glasgow
Carol Mathers, Fred Martin Project, Glasgow
Aileen Gibb, Barnardo's Family Support Team, Dundee
Christine Thompson, Barnardo's Family Support Team, Dundee.

USING VIDEO

Video can be a most valuable tool when it comes to educating communities about learning disabilities. Programmes can be shown to groups large and small, and even loaned to people for viewing at home.

- It provides opportunities for the public to 'meet' people;

- they can see examples of their talents in action;

- they can listen to them recounting their experiences;

- they can see good models of people interacting.

Through video, they can hear members of the public commenting on their reactions to people with disabilities. Video can also be used to 'teach' the public new skills, such as ways of conversing with people who have communication problems.

Video is also a tool which people who have learning disabilities can learn to use; enabling them to put across their feelings and experiences.

Unlike broadcast television, video programmes can reflect local situations and they can be tailored to the needs of different audiences. Video equipment is increasingly available at reasonable cost. A basic set would include a camcorder (preferably with remote microphone and tripod) and a second video recorder; costing around £1,000 new but this equipment would enable you to produce acceptable programmes.

However there are a growing number of video enthusiasts around who can share their expertise with novices. Likewise many secondary schools and Colleges offer media courses and have a fully equipped video studio. Students often undertake project work and local enthusiasts might be willing to do the work for you.

In this section we describe the programmes which could be made locally and suggestions for how to go about making them. Practical tips are given on the use of cameras and recorders, and on editing programmes.

Producing a Video Programme

A video-programme can take many forms. The simplest is playing back recordings, or parts of recordings you have made. No extra equipment is needed other than a camcorder/video-recorder and television. The recorder has a counter which enables you to identify the starting point of each sequence you wish to show. You can fast forward or rewind the tape to the starting point of each sequence you wish to show.

If you have access to a second recorder then you can edit your recordings into a programme (see later). This can be as simple or as complex as your time and equipment will permit. For example:

☐ **Picture Albums:** The easiest programme to make is simply an 'album' of the sequences you wish to show in the order you want them to appear but missing out all the unnecessary bits. You can provide the commentary as the group watches the pictures.

☐ **Soundtracks:** The next step is to add a commentary - soundtrack - to the pictures so that viewers can follow it without having a person present. For this, you need to have a recorder with an 'audio-dub' facility.

☐ **Programmes:** You can make your production more like a television programme by adding opening titles, music and captions. Access to an editing 'suite' makes this task a lot easier.

Programme styles

Two styles of programmes are useful in educating communities about learning disabilities.

1. Meeting people with disabilities and community representatives

In these programmes viewers have the chance to see and listen to people with learning disabilities. The emphasis should be on the people competently doing everyday things; e.g. a job of work or household tasks. The people should speak for themselves; hence it's better to use clear speakers. Show a number of different people in a variety of situations.

People from the community can also give their reactions to people with learning disabilities. Negative comments could be included to trigger discussions. People might also recount how their attitudes have changed. Again, try to have a variety of people in the 'programme'.

2. 'Instructional' programmes

Here the goal is to convey practical information primarily about how people might react with individuals who have a learning disability. Models of good practice should be shown although exaggerated 'bad' practice can be both funny and effective. It's best to emphasise three or four key points and follow-up the showing with discussion and suggested activities to reinforce the learning.

Another type of programme describes services on offer to people with learning disabilities. Although common, this sort of video production should be used with caution as it may unwittingly promote the service and the staff rather than portray positive images of people with learning disabilities and can fail to show how ordinary people can contribute to their lives.

Programme Making

The first step in making any programme is to decide on the group(s) at whom the programme is targeted and what are the messages you want to get across to them. The more focused the programme in terms of aims and audience, the more effective it is likely to be. However it may become so specialised that you rarely use it. Keeping a balance between specifics and general interest is quite an art!

Filming Plan

Whatever type of programme you aim to make, you need to plan in advance the video-recordings you will make. This is even more crucial if another person is going to operate the camera. He or she must know what to record and when to switch off. Otherwise you waste time and video-tape.

* Who are the people who need to appear in the programme? Aim to have a mix of people of different sexes, races, cultures and social classes.

* What visual images will convey your messages? Children playing a familiar game together shows integration in action. List as many examples as you can. If necessary bring along toys and playthings for use during the filming but use materials which are readily-available to the viewers.

* List the places where you can easily film, beginning with those you know personally. In our experience, people are pleased to appear on video. Even if you do not know them, try asking. It usually works.

* Try to visit the people you plan to film to explain what you want to do. This will also let you discover the best time and places for the recordings.

* Prepare a filming plan which notes what you want to record in each location be it a family home or a work place. Talk this over with the camera operator.

* Decide on the number of different locations you will use. The more you have the longer it will take. If your time is limited, record what you can in the time available and keep travel times to a minimum between locations.

During Filming

* When you arrive at the location set up the camera in the best position for filming. You will then know where to position the people.

* Try to have the video set-up and ready to record before bringing the children into the room. Do not let them 'play' with the camera. They may find this more interesting than what you want them to do!

* Your aim is to relax the people so that they behave as naturally as possible. Start with an activity they do often together or know well. Like when interviewing, get the people talking about themselves - the job they do, where they live etc.

* Do not get upset if things do not go as you plan. Suggest another attempt or move on to another activity from your list.

* Keep the camera running rather than pausing. Unlike film, video-tape can be re-used.

* When introducing a new activity, show the people what you want them to do. Telling is NOT enough. For example, you demonstrate the task, then ask the person to take over from you.

* If you are recording a number of different activities at the one location, change the setting if possible, e.g. child and mother on floor, sitting on chair, outside etc. You can also move the camera to give different backgrounds.

* If a crowd gathers to watch try to keep them out of sight of the people you are filming and ask them to be quiet. If they talk to the camera operator their voices will be heard in the microphone.

* Look out for other opportunities which arise during the filming. Sometimes the best things are those you didn't plan.

* Try to keep a log of what you have filmed on a note-pad - especially noting people's names.

* Record some general purpose shots - outside of homes, community scenes etc. These can be helpful when editing.

Making a Video Programme

The making of a video-programme can be taken in two parts. First, deciding on the content of the programme from the recordings you have made, i.e. the pictures and words to be used. Second, the technical operations involved in editing video recordings.

Again you might find it easier to leave the editing to a person who knows how to do this (The next section gives a basic introduction to editing). But as with the camera operator, the editor also needs a director to tell them what is to go into the programme. This is called writing a script.

Script-writing

This is like preparing a talk or writing a booklet. You first need to decide on the messages you want to get across to the viewer and the order in which they should be presented. This gives an overall structure for the programme.

○ Review all the recordings you have made; listings the ones which are suitable for use in the programme. Ideally these should clearly show the action you want and they are also technically good, i.e. in focus, not too far away; centred on the action. If they are technically poor it is better not to use them. Perhaps you could re-film?

○ Order the sequences as they will appear in the programme.

○ The lengths of the sequences you use can vary but beware of having them too long - the viewers can get bored. Equally they should not be too short. Viewers may not have time to recognise the action or they may not see all of it.

○ You will be able to judge the overall length of the programme by timing the different sequences you plan to use. Around 12 minutes is the maximum length for educational purposes. If the programme is going to be longer than this, break the programme into two parts.

○ You will need to write a commentary - to introduce certain sequences; to describe points the viewers should observe and to give additional information about the pictures, for example why an activity is particularly good for children to play. Keep your commentaries short and to the point. Use simple words and avoid describing what the viewer can see. A common mistake with inexperienced programme-makers is to include too much commentary. Let your pictures do the talking!

Using Video Equipment

This section gives further information about the technical aspects of using video-equipment. Two topics are covered:

- Using a video camera to make local recordings;

- Editing video-recordings into locally produced programmes

Using a Video Camera

A video camera lets you experience the real miracle of video at first hand. A scene you filmed a few minutes ago can be replayed instantly on a television. The past has not gone for ever. You can relive it at the touch of a button.

Video lets people see events they would not usually experience - children in school; families at play; people doing different jobs.

Modern cameras are compact, light-weight and easy to use. A video-tape will last for an hour or more; and they can be re-used. There are no developing costs as with still photographs.

But using a video camera to obtain training material, involves more than taking pictures. You need to have a plan for what you want to film as well as knowing how to use the camera.

Two people are better than one. The camera operator can then focus on getting good pictures while the second person is free to direct what is to be filmed. This section is more for the camera-operator; the next for the director.

Watch broadcast television programmes and news bulletins to pick up tips on using the camera - close-ups and wide shots, zooms in and out; panning shots - the camera swings round so that the viewers can see the whole scene, e.g. all the children in a classroom.

Before filming with a Camera

♦ Check that you have enough battery-power to do the filming - carry a spare battery or two with you.

♦ Check that you have enough video-tape.

♦ Check that the microphone is working and that it is switched on - use headphones.

♦ Check that the switches on the camera which control focus and light are in the correct position (see Handbook for camera). On modern cameras you can usually use the 'automatic' settings.

♦ Make a test recording and play it back to check the standard of recordings. The extra few minutes spent doing this is time well spent, especially for beginners.

During Filming

♦ Reduce background noise to a minimum - ask for radios to be switched off or turned down.

♦ It is easier to film out-of-doors in the shade. Try to do this as much as possible.

♦ You should film with the main source of light behind the camera. If you film into the light, people's faces are darkened.

♦ If filming indoors, select a bright room; switch on any electric lights; position the people close to a window but have the window behind or to the side of the camera. Some cameras are fitted with a 'gain' switch which boosts darker scenes.

♦ A common mistake is to film a scene without having pressed the RECORD button on the camera; hence nothing gets recorded. Get into the habit of checking that the REC signal appears in the camera viewfinder.

♦ When filming, the general rule-of-thumb is to fill the screen with the action. This could mean a shot of just one person (a child playing alone); two people (child being fed) or three and more. Likewise when interviewing people use mainly a head and shoulders shot.

♦ Avoid constantly zooming in and out. Have a count of at least ten seconds between zooms.

♦ Move the camera slowly and steadily when panning around a scene. Decide your start and stop points in advance and hold them for at least 10 seconds.

♦ Close-ups of people's faces; actions they are doing with their hands and so on, make good television and help the viewer to see more of what is going on. Hold the close-ups for a count of at least 10 seconds. Try to have three different close-ups in each scene - of the child; the parent and objects they are using. You may have to ask the people to repeat the activity so that you can film it again, only this time in close-ups rather than wide shots.

♦ Wide shots are useful when editing the material and they help viewers get an overall idea of where the activity is taking place. For example, a wide view of children playing outside the house.

♦ Keep an eye open for interesting camera angles, e.g. having the camera on the floor in front of a child who is crawling. These make more interesting television.

♦ Recording sound is the hardest part of video. Microphones pick up a lot extra noise - traffic and wind are the most common. Hence try to find a quieter place out of the wind!

♦ Do not switch the camera off during the recordings; use the pause or the stand-by switch. When the camera is switched off, it rewinds the tape by around 10 seconds; hence you will lose part of your recordings as you switch off. Likewise do not stop filming as soon as the action stops. Let the camera run on for at least 10 seconds before you switch off.

Recording Interviews

♦ Use a clip-on neck microphone - the sound is much clearer and background noise is minimised.

♦ Use the quietest place available. Turn off fans and air-conditioners; tell other people to be quiet or ask them to leave.

♦ Check the background; use a situation which is natural for that person to be in, e.g. parents in a homely setting.

♦ Dark-skinned people should be filmed against a dark background - otherwise their faces are cast into shadow.

♦ Do not have the person looking directly at the camera; they might talk to a person to one side of the camera.

♦ Use head and shoulder shots in the main; vary with close-ups of their face and possibly a wide shot that also shows the interviewer. Avoid zooming in or out when the person is talking. Make the adjustments when questions are being asked or take a pause while you adjust the camera.

♦ During editing, it is easier if you record all the interviews on one tape and on another tape, any scenes you want to use to illustrate the interview.

After Recording

♦ To save time, we generally do not show people everything which we have recorded. It is possible to show short extracts through the camera view-finder.

♦ Label the video-tape so that you can find the recordings again.

♦ Video-tapes are fitted with a 'tab' which when broken off or switched to a certain position, prevents new recordings being made. This is a useful safety feature.

♦ As you watch your recordings, identify good and bad shots. You will soon find out how you can improve your camera techniques.

Making Video Programmes

Video-tape cannot be cut and reassembled to make a programme. As we are dealing with electrical signals, you have to make copies of those you want on to another tape. This is known in video jargon as editing. To do this you will need a second video-recorder, preferably one with an editing facility that enables the signals from two recordings to be joined smoothly on the copy tape. Use High Grade Tapes for your programmes; the extra money buys better picture quality.

Editing can be done quickly if you only have two or three scenes to join. The more sequences you have the longer it takes. Three other factors are important in determining the time it will take to make programmes. First, your familiarity with the recordings, so that you can quickly find the sequences you want to use in the programmes. Second, how practised you are in the mechanics of editing - again, you will improve with practice. Third, the type of equipment you use. Some of the recent, but sadly more expensive machines, make editing so much easier.

A rough rule of thumb, is that it can take one hour to produce two minutes of finished programmes. It is a time-consuming job and you can begin to appreciate the large teams of people needed to produce television programmes. However it may be possible to get people to do the job for you - such as students taking video courses in secondary schools or colleges.

Setting up the editing equipment The equipment needed to edit is listed earlier. You have to link one recorder to another using special leads.

○ Use the video lead to link the video out socket on the camcorder (i.e. this plays back recordings) to the Video In socket on the video-recorder (one which you will record the programme).

○ Use the audio lead to link the Audio Out socket on the camcorder to the Audio In socket on the video-recorder.

○ Connect the television to the video-recorder (via RF lead or preferably by video and audio leads if using a video monitor.)

When you play tapes in the camcorder, they will show on the television if the second video-recorder is switched on and left in Stop or Record Pause.

Tips on editing

○ Leave at least one minute of blank tape at the beginning of the programme master. This part of the tape gets most wear and tear through use; hence it is best left blank or you get picture interference.

○ You can get a smooth start to the programme by having the first sequence as a blank screen. To do this, leave the lens cap on the camera and record about one minute of blank.

○ The basic steps involved in editing one sequence are

1. Find the point on the programme tape where the edit should begin. Put the recorder into Pause and press RECORD button.

2. On the camcorder find the point where you want the sequence to start in your programme.

3. Rewind for at least 10 seconds and put the camcorder into pause. You are now ready to do the edit.

4. Release the pause on the camcorder and when it comes close to the start point, release the pause on the video-recorder. This machine will start copying the sequence on the programme tape. When you come to the end of the sequence, press pause on the video-recorder. You can then stop the camcorder.

5. You can check the edit, by coming out of the RECORD mode in the video-recorder and playing back the newly recorded sequence. In particular, you should check that the join at the start of the edit is smooth - the picture does not jump or distort. Should this happen you can re-do the edit.

6. You repeat the above 5 steps for every edit which you make. In this way the programme is slowly built up.

Video-recorders have a three second delay from releasing the pause button until they start recording. This may explain why the start of some sequences in your programme are missing. The solution is simple, release the pause about three seconds before you want the sequence to start.

○ Thus far you have been performing what is known as Assembly edit. Each sequence is linked to the one before. This is the most straightforward method but it has a big drawback. With this method you cannot go back and redo an earlier sequence, or change them around.

○ To do this, you need a recorder that can do INSERT editing. Here you can drop a new sequence into the middle of an existing one or between two existing sequences. This needs more sophisticated equipment although many recent models have this facility. The handbook of the recorders will give you further details of the many advantages of this form of editing.

○ You also need to attend to the sound during editing. On the video-recorder you should be able to adjust the level of the sound that is recorded. This should be low at the beginning of a sequence and increased over the first two or three seconds of the sequence. Likewise it is good to fade the sound down at the end of the sequence. This gives a more professional finish to your edits.

You should also keep the recorded sound low, if a commentary is to be added. Thus during the edit, read the commentary and when the section is finished increase the sound. This means that there will be no sudden changes in sound levels during the programme.

Recording Commentaries or Music

☐ You need a camcorder/video-recorder which has an audio-dub button.

☐ Link the microphone or tape-recorder to the video-recorder.

☐ Identify the point in the programme where the first audio-dub comes. Press PAUSE and AUDIO-DUB buttons. When you release the PAUSE, the audio-dubbing will start. With music, fade it in and out by using the sound levels controls on the video-recorder.

☐ When you come to the end of the sequence, promptly press PAUSE or STOP on the video-recorder, otherwise the audio-dub will continue and you may lose other sounds from the programme. Remember, an audio-dub wipes out the original sound on the programme.

☐ If you are not happy with the sound recording you can easily do them again. However the new recording needs to 'wipe out' the old one; thus the audio-dub must be at least the same length as the previous take.

As with all new skills the more you practice, the more polished will become your performance. Happy filming and viewing!

Further Information

Video Programmes are available on loan from:

Barnardo's Film Library, Tanner's Lane, Barkingside, Ilford, Essex IG6 1QC

Concord Film and Film Council, 201 Felixstowe Road, Ipswich, Suffolk IP3 9BJ

Mental Health Media, Resource Centre, 356 Holloway Road, London N7 6PA

Scottish Film and Video Library, 74 Victoria Crescent, Govanhill, Glasgow G12 8JN

SURVEYING COMMUNITY ATTITUDES

Consulting with local communities is the best foundation on which to build a caring community. So obvious is that statement it must rank as a truism, yet future historians of social policy will look back in amazement that so many community care initiatives in the 1990s ignored this simple truth. Little wonder that today, so many of our services are located in communities but they are not part of the community. This is vividly illustrated by surveys of people living adjacent to services and being unaware of their existence (see p. 16).

One excuse for this state of affairs is that service providers are so preoccupied with meeting the needs of their clients that they have done little to nurture the resources or skills required to consult with the community.

In an attempt to rectify this, the Educating Communities Network organised a workshop for members on carrying out local surveys and from this several groups undertook their own projects; the results of which were given earlier.

This section contains a beginner's guide to surveying community attitudes and draws on the experiences of Network members on so doing. But first we begin by examining some of the good reasons for finding out the attitudes of people locally.

Why survey attitudes?

By obtaining information directly from local people, you will be able to -

• Detect their concerns and target your educational initiatives more precisely.

• Discover possible 'allies' who could support greater community involvement.

• Document the balance of opinion on controversial issues, such as group homes opening in the locality.

A survey can also be an educational tool in itself. Issues about learning disabilities are brought to the public's attention; information leaflets can be left with them; their questions can be answered and any misconceptions corrected. In sum, a survey starts a dialogue.

More ambitious surveys can produce further outcomes. You can -

• gain a greater understanding of who are the people most disposed to helping and those who may prove most antagonistic.

• evaluate changes in people's attitudes and identify the factors which contributed to the change.

Finally, by making your findings available to other people, e.g. service personnel, social work officials, local councillors, you will enhance your credibility. Proposals for action carry more weight when backed with facts and figures.

Of course it is possible to draw upon the results of surveys carried out elsewhere. However these are still few in number and as we shall see later, the results may not hold for your own locality. There is really no substitute to sampling local opinion!

Stereotyping People with Learning Disabilities

A cogent criticism of social surveys is that they lump people together by labels and may unwittingly reinforce stereotypes. Moreover, the group who is the focus of the survey may feel strongly that they should not be singled out for attention in this way and yet they are powerless to prevent it.

These arguments are all the stronger when it is presumed the results will portray negative opinions of the labelled group, be it 'the Labour Party'; 'the police' or 'people with mental handicaps'.

The benefits of doing a survey must outweigh its dangers and this judgement has to be made anew for each proposed survey. For example, a survey of playgroup leaders with Downs Syndrome children in their groups may yield information that could encourage other leaders to enrol similar children.

Likewise possible dangers can be minimised by the design of the survey. First by balancing the questions so that positive opinions can also be expressed. Hence enquiries can be made about the benefits as well as problems of having a child with disabilities in the classroom. Second, the use of language throughout the questionnaire should be non-stigmatising; e.g. referring to people 'who have been labelled as having a learning disability'. Third, information leaflets can be left at the end of the interviews to counteract any stereotypes or apprehensions. In neighbourhood surveys, for example, these would stress that house values do not drop when houses open.

Perhaps the best safeguard of all is to ensure that people with disabilities and/or their advocates are also included in the planning of any surveys (see p. 152).

Central Concerns

In order to measure accurately the attitudes of any community - be it school pupils,factory employees or the public at large - three core issues have to be addressed.

☐ First, the issue of *representativeness;* are the results obtained typical of all the people who belong to that particular community?

☐ Second, the issue of *measurement;* which particular measures do you include, given the variety of types presently available?

☐ Third, the issue of *validity;* do people's verbal responses correspond with how they will actually behave?

As we will see, completely satisfactory answers to these three questions are difficult to obtain, especially in view of the scarce resources available to service personnel. It may be some comfort to know that even well-endowed researchers, whose efforts have been published in reputable journals, have often ignored one or all of these items. This explains many of the contradictions found in the literature, some of which should be treated as examples of what not to do!

Of course, a central obstacle to precise measurement is the vagueness of the term 'attitudes'. Much psychological debate still rages over this but for our purposes, I shall take it to mean people's expressed opinions and their anticipated reactions towards specific events which have occurred, or may occur, within their personal experience.

My primary focus will also be on surveys based around self-completed questionnaires and structured, face-to-face interviews with individuals. This is not to belittle other approaches, such as in-depth interviews with key people or direct observations of people's behaviour, but these methods are often more demanding in the time needed for data collection and analysis. To date, they have been rarely used for exploring attitudes to people with disabilities.

Representativeness of Samples

In designing any survey the starting point is to identify the community, or communities whose views you wish to examine. Communities can be defined geographically, or more relevantly as people sharing a common interest or experience, such as first year pupils in secondary schools, shopkeepers in a town or playgroup leaders throughout the county. In either case these form the *population* to be studied.

The next step is to decide how specific you want this population to be. Let us take the first year school pupils. Do you need to know the attitudes of all first years in only one particular school, or do you want to draw conclusions that apply to all first years throughout the Region?

Once you can estimate the likely number of people in the target population, decisions can then be made about the sample you use for the study. If you have chosen only one school, and the school is a small one, then the sampling problem is solved straightaway. You should aim to obtain responses from all first year pupils and not bother sampling.

If however, the population is larger (over 200 say) it is more efficient to *sample* the views of a smaller number of people; the theory being that this will come up with the same results, than if you included everyone from the population.   But there is a very important proviso; the sample chosen must be representative of its population.

National opinion polls are a case in point. A sample of just over 1,000 people can accurately represent the views of all British adults and despite politicians' protestations, most reputable polling agencies produce highly reliable findings.   That is two different samples drawn from the same population will come up with identical findings albeit within a stated margin of error, say plus or minus 3%.   Conversely, samples which are unrepresentative will not give accurate results.

How then can you be sure the sample you use is representative? The preferred method is to draw the people at random from the population. For example putting the names of all first year pupils into a hat and drawing out your sample at random.   A less cumbersome method would be to take every third or fifth name from the school registers of first years; depending on the size your sample needs to be.   A similar procedure can be used to draw names from the electoral register when doing a neighbourhood survey.

The number of people making up your sample is not chosen arbitrarily but rather is set by a statistical formulae which calculates the sample size for populations of known numbers. The table below gives you an idea of sample sizes within a 5% margin of error. As you can see, the larger the population becomes, the sample becomes proportionately smaller.

Population	Sample
250	115
500	170
750	205
1,000	230
2,000	280
5,000	335
10,000	360

When it is not possible to list all the population to draw a random sample, an alternative is to use a *quota sample*. For this, you need pertinent details about the structure of the population, such as age and sex. You then divide the sample into the numbers - or quotas - of people of each sex and in each age band you need to include in the study so that you mirror the population. You now can take people as they come along, rather than selecting randomly in advance, until you have all the quotas filled. So in a factory workforce of 500 people, you know that 70% are women and 30% men; and also that 60% of workers are under 30 years. The sample of 172 should be made up of the following quotas:

	Women	*Men*
Under 30	72	31
30 yrs. +	48	21
Totals:	120	52

Books on survey techniques will contain more information about sampling (see Further Reading).

Selecting Measures

People's characteristics - such as their age, their ethnic origin and
if they have a relative who has Down's Syndrome - can all be
measured in some way or other. The three examples listed are
relatively straightforward to measure and can be done in a variety
of ways. Age for example can be done by asking their birth year
and getting a precise numbers; or by having them indicate a
particular age band. Ethnic origin could be measured most simply
as either British and non-British, or by having seven categories
reflecting a range of ethnic backgrounds.

Rating Scales But how do you measure other features of people,
such as their reactions to people who have learning disabilities or
their willingness to help? A favoured option is the use of rating
scales. For example, people can rate their agreement to statements
such as: 'If a group of people with learning disabilities moved into
your neighbourhood, how willing would you be ... to visit their
house. Three alternatives can be provided such as: 'Yes
definitely; Yes maybe, Prefer not'. A five point or seven point
scale can also be used with intermediate points not named but
marked by dots, viz.

	Definitely Yes					*Definitely Not*
Visit their Home	●	●	●	●	●	●	●

Such scales it is argued, are more sensitive to small change's in
people's attitudes but by the same token, they are also less reliable
in that people vary their ratings without any genuine change of
attitude. Likert scales of this type, as they are known, are better
used in written questionnaires.

Some information can be obtained by measures which are a
mixture of fact and ratings. A popular one in our researches has
been: 'What contact have you had in the past with people who

have learning disabilities - No contact; Just seen them around; Occasional meetings or chats; Close regular contact.

Selecting Questions   Thus far we have dealt with different types of measures but more crucial is deciding which measures to use in your own survey?   The questions you pose all derive from the aims of your survey, namely what information do you want to know and why?   The answers to these questions should be spelt out in as much detail as possible and debated by all the members of the group involved.

In our work we have found four types of questions to be informative; namely questions which ask about:

  1: past/present contact with people who have a
       learning disability;
  2: knowledge of learning disabilities and local facilities;
  3: reactions to further contact; concerns and anticipated
       problems;
  4: willingness for involvement.

Devising Questions   The next stage is to cast the information in the form of questions which you could use in the survey.   For example, if you wanted to know what concerns employers had about taking a person with learning disabilities on to their workforce you might ask what is called an 'open' question: viz. "If you were asked to take a person with learning disabilities on work experience placements for two days a week, do you think this would give rise to any problems?   Irrespective as to whether the person answers 'yes' or 'no', they are then asked to state the reason for their answer.

Alternatively a number of specific concerns could be put to them (drawn from past research) and the employers asked to state whether or not that would concern them.   These close questions have the advantage of being quicker to answer; the results are easier to analyse and they prompt respondents to think of relevant concerns which they otherwise forget to mention. The downside is that not every conceivable concern can be listed in advance and you may then miss some important concerns which local people have. Hence most questionnaires use a combination of open and closed questions.

Wording Questions   The wording of questions can have an important influence on the response you get from people. Hence care should be taken to avoid possible biases or confused responses.   Among the most common faults in questions are the use of negatives, obtuse words and phrases (mental handicap might be preferable to 'learning disabilities'); and asking people to think of hypothetical situations.   Generally the more specific and personal the question is to respondents the more likely they are to give consistent and comprehensible replies.   Examining the questions used in past surveys is an excellent way of findings one suitable for your own survey.

Pilot Testing Once a preliminary set of questions is drawn up for the survey, you can try them out on colleagues or friends. Their reactions will soon tell you which questions require to be changed. A common complaint is asking too many questions and/or ones which seem very similar.

The re-drafted questionnaire should then be tried out with a small group of people from the target population. This will be a further check on the questions and also give you a flavour of the information which you will obtain. If this is not what you expected you may have to do further re-drafting of questions or include new ones.

Attitudes and Behaviour

Finally, we come to the crunch question - will people behave the way they say they will behave? A great deal of attitudinal research has been based on the presumption that they will. But at the same time, our world experience tells us that people frequently say one thing and do another. There are a number of steps which you can take to reduce the likelihood of a mismatch but it can be never be eliminated. The attitudes we aim to measure are those expressed towards a general class of people (i.e. with learning disabilities) with broad contexts in mind (i.e. reactions to people living in the neighbourhood), whereas behaviours are often triggered by particular individuals in specific situations.

The wording of questions can go a long way to ensuring that respondents' expressed attitudes are a reflection of the way they would behave. Four other steps can be taken.

Past Contacts A person's previous behaviour us likely to be the best single predictor of their future behaviour. It is therefore important in any study to include questions about the extent of the person's past and present contacts with people who have learning disabilities. At the very least this will let you separate out those who 'know what they are talking about' from those with no direct experience. Our past research confirms that previous contacts do predict willingness to help.

Specific actions A second approach is to present the respondents with a number of specific courses of action to ascertain how likely they might be to pursue each one. By inviting people to share their 'behavioural intentions' we are more likely to correctly predict the actions they could take. For example, in a survey carried out in Israel into reactions to community housing, people were presented with 42 possible courses of actions, including "sign a letter of protest; donate money to remove retarded persons and look for an alternative house". Four distinct patterns of reactions emerged in a survey of over 400 people suggesting that different strategies might be needed to induce attitude changes in the different groups.

Likewise in our Scottish surveys we have included a range of specific suggestions as to how people might be willing to help (see p. 22). This gives people the chance to state an unwillingness without appearing to be uncaring. The latter is known as 'socially acceptable answers'.

Picturing Reality People's expressed intentions may not translate into action simply because they do not believe such experiences will ever happen to them. Hence, American researchers found that the number of potential objectors to group homes increased three-fold when researchers pointed out an empty house in an estate and implied that it was to become a group home. Likewise in our surveys we found that people living in an area with an existing group home were less likely to anticipate problems for neighbours than did people living in areas with no home. The moral is clear: much more accurate and meaningful information is obtained if people are asked to comment on situations which are real to them.

Observe their behaviours Finally, direct observations of people's behaviours is much more reliable than seeking their predictions as to how they think they would behave. However this option is rarely possible in group-based surveys which aim to provide a snap-shot at a point in time. But reports of people's behaviours can form an important element in determining the success of educational initiatives; for example the number of people who attend an information session on a new befriending scheme.

Equally valuable in designing educational inputs can be the reports of people's behaviour provided by individuals with disabilities who have been at the receiving end of their jibes and abuse.

Carrying Out Surveys

Having decided who is to be included in the survey and the questions to be asked a number of other key decisions remain. First, how will the information be obtained, who can help with collecting it and how will the data be analysed?

Collecting Information: The two most popular methods have been self-completed questionnaires and personal interviews. A third possibility is the use of telephone surveys but they run of the risk of giving biased samples.

The main advantage of self-completion questionnaires is that large numbers of people can be included in the sample yet the information can be obtained in a relatively short space of time. Among the disadvantages is the poor return when questionnaires are sent by post; typically only 30% of people reply. However this figure can be increased by delivering the questionnaire and arranging to collect it personally.

Personal interviews are however the preferred method of collecting information and is much used by market researchers and opinion pollsters.   This is more likely to generate a higher participation rate and hence a representative sample is more likely to be obtained.   The interview can also include a wider range of questions, especially open questions which yield more qualitative answers.   The downside is the amount of time and/or personnel needed to undertake even a small number of interviews.

Obtaining Interviewers   Market research agencies will carry out local, regional and national surveys according to their customer's specifications.   Assuming that the finance is not available to do this; a most likely scenario I suspect, all is not lost.   In the surveys undertaken by members of the Educating Communities Network, a range of helpers were recruited (see p. 13).

In one survey a part-time worker was employed to do the bulk of the work alongside some workers from the service.   In three surveys, students on placements from universities acted as interviewers and survey co-ordinators.   In another, volunteer helpers were recruited via an advertisement in a local newspaper. Finally, the neighbourhood survey in Dundee was done by the staff and some service-users from the resource centre (see p. 152).

Irrespective of who makes up the team of interviewers, it is crucial that they are briefed and trained so that the same procedures are followed.   Interviewer bias is a well known phenomena.   For example, the same explanation should be given as to why the study is being carried out and all questions should be delivered with consistent wording and emphasis.

Analysing the results   Even a modest questionnaire with fifteen questions if given to 100 people, generates 1,500 bits of information!   In order to make sense of it all, the results have to be summarised.   By far the most convenient way of doing this is by personal computer although those with time and patience could do it by hand! Spreadsheets and statistical packages such as SPSS will quickly provide a breakdown of the sample's responses to each question. More sophisticated analysis can provide yet more detailed replies; for example the opinions of those who had prior contact with those in the sample who have had no contact.

Once again, university students and their lecturers may assist with the data analysis but make sure you approach them before you start collecting the information. Data analysis is so much easier if it has been planned for when devising the questions and in laying out the questionnaire.

Sharing the Results

The last step is the most crucial. The information obtained in the survey needs to be shared with colleagues and those who participated in the study. Sadly the latter are often forgotten! The most popular method is the written report but for this to have maximum impact it needs to be short and to the point, with the data given in charts and graphs as these are much easier to read than columns of figures.

Local newspaper and magazine articles based on the survey results will reach a wider audience and you might be saved the trouble of writing them if you can interest local reporters in your findings. But it is essential that you check their articles before they appear in print.

Is All the Work Worth It?

Surveys do require a lot of work. The efforts expended on them may not be justified, especially if there is no energy or resources left to undertake any educational endeavours. But as we said at the outset, community care schemes are implemented with the minimum of information about communities and with little effort to engage them in the process. Surveys are but one response to bridging this gap.

Further Reading

Hoinville, G., Jowell, R. and associates (1978). *Survey Research Practice,* Heinemann Educational Books, London.

Fink, A. and Kosecoff, J. (1985). *How to conduct surveys: A step-by-step guide.* Sage Publications, California. by

Munn, P. and Drever, E. (1990). *Using Questionnaires in Small-scale Research: A Teachers' Guide,* Edinburgh, Scottish Council for Educational Research.

These books provide an excellent guide to beginners wishing to learn how to conduct various kinds of surveys. They are very readable and contain plenty of examples.

Workshop Participants

Philip Russell, Elcap, East Lothian
Lisa Mills, Elcap, East Lothian
Julie Ridley, Tayside Regional Social Work Department
Pamela Robbie, Kemback Street Resource Centre, Dundee
Stewart Robertson, Quarrier's Home Life Project, Glasgow
Robert Darroch, Quarrier's Home Life Project, Glasgow
Debbie Woods, Action Group, Edinburgh
Diane Steel, Action Group, Edinburgh
Pat Stevenson, Barnardo's Advocacy Service, Tayside
Alison McGilvray, Scottish Down's Syndrome Association

EVALUATING THE IMPACT OF COMMUNITY INITIATIVES

Educating communities about learning disability is a new endeavour. As yet we are slowly building up experience and expertise in doing this. This process will be enhanced if practitioners take time to evaluate the impact of their initiatives. Valuable information will then be obtained as to what works and what has not worked. Passing on this knowledge to colleagues will make their job easier; whether they be working locally or in another part of the country.

As with many other desirable tasks, it is easier to talk about its merits than to put it into practice. In this section, we draw together some tips for busy community educators to make evaluation a more manageable undertaking for themselves. In this instance; any feedback from communities is better than none.

The guest for the workshop on this theme was:

☼ Julie Ridley, Research and Information Section, Social Work Department, Tayside Regional Council, Dundee

Two Outcomes from Evaluation

Evaluations can yield two complementary types of information. Confusion (and disappointment) can reign if people expect one type but are given another.

* *Formative evaluations:* The aim here is to discover the successes and limitations of the educational initiative. This in turn should lead to improvements to its style and format. An example would be asking the viewers of a video programme which you have produced to give their reactions to it and suggestions for improvements.

* *Summative evaluations* aim to demonstrate the outcomes of the initiative and discover whether it is more or less effective than other approaches at increasing their knowledge, changing their attitudes and influencing their behaviour. So for example in this instance, the video viewers might be given a test of the knowledge to see what they have learnt from the programme; asked to complete questionnaires regarding their attitudes and records kept of the number of people who volunteered to become a helper at a social club. If similar information was obtained from groups who had heard a lecture on similar topics, then the relative effectiveness of each approach could be described.

In general, service practitioners are usually more interested in the first, whereas service planners and funders often want answers to the second. Ideally, an evaluation would embrace both types but when time and resources are limited, priority may have to be given to one rather than to another.

Evaluation is Research

At heart, evaluation is a research endeavour; finding out, in an objective a way as possible, people's reactions to the educational initiative and /or the effect the initiative had on people's knowledge, attitudes and behaviour. Ideally, experienced evaluators or researchers might undertake this task for you but if they cannot be found, then yet again, self-help becomes the antidote to inaction.

Three features of a research approach are worth stressing as they can easily be overlooked by busy educators. These are:

■ **Objectivity** Research strives to produce reliable and precise information. On the whole this is more easily attained by using some form of objective measurement that is open to independent confirmation and scrutiny rather than reliance on practitioner's judgements and opinions. This can be a major culture shock to long-serving professionals who expect their opinions to be treated as facts!

■ **Systematic procedures** Research demands that the same measures are collected and the same procedures used across all the people involved in the project. Once again, the aim is to reduce biases creeping into the results.

■ **Plan of action** Research is a process rather than a product. It consists of a set of aims; the execution of a number of tasks in order to achieve those aims within a given time-period, an assessment of the implications of the outcomes and recommendations for future action. In sum, research is an activity that has to be planned well in advance rather than done on the spur of the moment.

Research Myths Equally there are a number of myths about research which need to be dispelled. First, the myth that research produces proof; e.g. you can 'prove' that one intervention is more cost-effective than another. Given the crudeness of our measures and methods for describing human behaviour, at best our research is better thought of as accruing evidence to support certain beliefs.

Another myth is thinking that there is only one way by which the impact can be adequately assessed. Hence if you do not have the time and resources to undertake the 'ideal' evaluation then a feasible alternative is to use methods and approaches with which you can cope; the dictum being that any research is better than none.

A third myth is the complexity of research methods and that only specialist researchers are capable of coping with this undertaking. Admittedly there are important pitfalls to be avoided but on the whole, a great deal of information can be obtained using simple methods which can be quickly mastered by others.

Essentials to Evaluation

Experience has identified a number of key elements in undertaking effective evaluations of community initiatives. These are:

* A clear statement is needed as to the aims and goals which the initiative is trying to meet. This will provide a yardstick for the evaluation and should ensure that all aspects of the initiative are covered. The most common mistake here is to expect too much from the one project.

* Involve all the stake-holders. Evaluations are stronger if all the people involved in the initiative, or likely to be have been affected by it are given the opportunity to participate. For example, as well as getting the views of school children to an integrated playscheme, you could also obtain the reactions of their teachers, the views of the children with disabilities whom they met and the opinions of these children's parents to the project.

* Evaluation can be on-going. Regular checks can be taken throughout the project, including at the end of each planning meeting or following each contact session. The evaluation can then become a learning - and possibly team-building - experience.

* Basic factual information is available about the participants - numbers, ages, sex etc. - and a clear description is prepared of what happened during the educational initiative, e.g. the topics covered in discussion with the Resident's Association.

Information Gathering

Throughout any initiative, the people involved in it are constantly evaluating how it is going. Their feelings and opinions are often used to shape the project as it unfolds and rightly so. However what if they get it wrong or are blind to certain key aspects? Feedback from the participants is crucial. This can be done in various ways.

○ Listening to people talking as you chat informally with them during a coffee break;

○ A group discussion at the end of a session in which people describe what they liked about the session and what they would do differently next time;

○ Likewise, people can complete a short written questionnaire giving their reactions to the same two questions noted above, with space provided for any further comments;

○ A selection of participants can be interviewed individually and preferably by a person who was not involved with the initiative.

All these methods will generate useful information which will help you to shape the community initiative to better suit the needs of the participants. They are also useful for obtaining people's views as to how their perceptions of disability have changed.

However, more formal evaluations are often expected when it comes to assessing the outcomes of the initiative, i.e. summative evaluation. The main difference is the greater use of objective measures to determine what, if anything, has changed. The most usual methods for doing this are self-completed questionnaires or individual interviews which explore participants' knowledge, attitudes and behaviours (see p. 217).

These approaches have a number of advantages:

● A structured questionnaire covers issues which might otherwise be overlooked in informal discussion;

● Basic information is gathered which is open to cross-checking and enables comparisons to be made more easily, for example with information collected in other studies.

● Information can be collected at various points in time so that changes in people's perceptions can be more easily monitored.

Monitoring Changes

Surveying people's perceptions at the end of an educational initiative can be informative but does not count as a measure of change. For example, a high degree of willingness to help may have been present at the outset and hence the initiative produced no change.

Additional measures are needed in order to monitor change.

Pre-post comparisons As the name suggests, the same measures are taken on two occasions. Hence this design can identify the extent of changes in people's knowledge, opinions and reported behaviours. Moreover, changes on certain measures but not in others can help to pinpoint the specific impact of initiatives. For example, when we contrasted the opinions of neighbours before, and two years after a facility opened in their neighbourhood we found that many of the anticipated concerns had evaporated - threat to children; that people with learning disabilities would be teased and so on. But one concern had actually increased, namely the people in the facility were isolated from the rest of the neighbours.

Contrast Groups Most often this involves having a 'control' group of people who do not participate in the initiative so that change is inferred by contrasting the results of the two groups. Although this approach is popular in the biological and medical sciences, it is fraught with problems for the social researcher, not least because of difficulties in arriving at two comparable groupings.   However a weaker form of this design can prove useful by contrasting naturally occurring groupings, e.g. reactions of school children which has pupils with special needs integrated in classes and a school where integration has not taken place.

A mixture of these two approaches can produce a very powerful way of determining change while also identifying if the change can be replicated and maintained; two aspects often ignored by investigators. The features of this approach are outlined in the Figure below but this research design requires a lot of planning and is best done in the context of specific research projects.

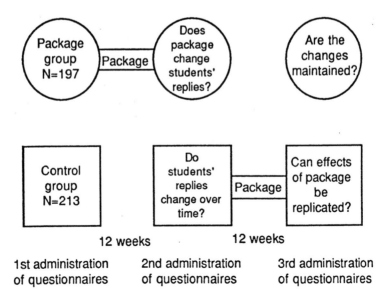

In this design, two groups of people are formed; one of which experiences the educational package while the other acts as a 'control'. However both groups complete questionnaires before and after the package is used. In the next phase, the group which had acted as control now also experiences the package. Then both groups are given the questionnaires for a third time. By comparing the results of the two groups at various points in time, the extent of change in people's attitudes can be assessed as the Figure illustrates.

Longitudinal Studies These entail making repeated measurements over a period of time (hence the alternative name of 'time-series'), usually of particular behaviours. Weight-watchers will recognise the value of this design in determining whether their diet is having an effect. Indeed this design is the only one which produces sensitive measures of trends and changes. With it causal links can be identified and checked and individual variability allowed for. Practitioners are uniquely placed to provide longitudinal data on clients but obsessive record-keeping is a prerequisite and as the volume of information grows the danger increases that it never gets analysed. To date, there have been few if any longitudinal studies of changes in people's attitudes.

Obtaining Assistance with Research

If you have stayed with me thus far, I have tried to show how practitioners can tailor their evaluation to suit the resources at their disposal. In this section I want to briefly outline the assistance often available to them but rarely accessed.

● **Access to, and reading of, journals, research reports etc.**
These provide example of methods as well as highlighting important factors to be considered in planning evaluations.

● **Access to 'research expertise'.** Knowing people locally with whom you can discuss the evaluation of projects is a big asset. Try to track them down; there are more around than you might think. Sometimes even explaining to a colleague the problem you have encountered may in itself let you see solutions.

● **Access to 'research assistants'.** Unlike the popular image of researchers undertaking exciting, even dangerous tasks, much of the work is sheer drudgery! Sharing the burdens with students on placement, secretarial staff, part-time paid helpers and even voluntary workers can help.

● **Access to personal computers** Learning to use word-processing packages along with data handling programmes such as databases and spreadsheets can make research much more feasible to undertake. This could help with many other aspects of your work!

Of course other service developments have much to contribute - the provision of training courses in research geared to the needs of practitioners and opportunities for service staff to take such courses; new styles of research degrees which foster practitioner based research skills; and the creation of a development post within a service (even for short time-periods) to free a member of staff to undertake a specific project.

But rather than waiting for these developments to occur, practitioners may have to earn them by undertaking research within existing resources and demonstrating its value to service development and delivery.

Personal Qualities

Finally are some people better-suited to being evaluators than others? Various writers believe so and for what it's worth I pass on their conclusions:

☐ Questioning person - not satisfied with the status quo
☐ Creative - enjoys thinking of new approaches
☐ Risk-taker - prepared to discover uncomfortable truths
☐ Good Manager/Planner - at best, research is nine-tenths routine management and one-tenth inspiration
☐ Diplomat and good communicator - to smooth negotiations with the many people involved
☐ Numerate - comfortable at handling and interpreting numbers
☐ Plodder - once embarked upon the project is willing to keep going until it is finished.

Obviously, all these qualities are unlikely to be found in the same person, especially as some appear contradictory. They can however, all be found in a team of two or three people with complementary talents. Hence a final tip for budding researchers - find a partner or partners to do it with!

Is It Worth It?

By now you may feel that evaluation is way beyond your meagre resources and be tempted to leave it to others. Can I ask you to think again? When all is said and done, the most convincing reason for evaluating our work, however humbly, is the positive feedback which it invariably provides for the people who instigated the project. This in turn is crucial for maintaining their enthusiasm for educating communities. Otherwise the danger is that it becomes an extra chore.

Further Reading

Kane, E. (1985). *Doing your own research*, Dublin, Turoe Press.

Whitaker, D.S. and Archer, J.L. (1989). *Research by Social Workers: Capitalizing on Experience*, London, Central Council for Education and Training in Social Work.

SECTION 4
RESOURCES FOR EDUCATING COMMUNITIES

Information is the kernel of education. In recent years there has been a burgeoning of print, video and packaged training materials. Throughout the book, particular resources have been listed. In this Section, the addresses of a range of organisations are provided. They provide various types of resource materials and further details of what they offer can be obtained on request.

Barnardo's
Tanners Lane,
Barkingside
Ilford,
Essex IG6 1QG

British Epilepsy Association
40, Hanover Square
Leeds LS3 1BE

British Institute of Learning Disabilities,
Wolverhampton Road,
Kidderminister DY10 3PP
Worcs., England

Centre for Studies in Integrated Education (CSIE)
4th Floor
415 Edgware Road,
London NW2 6NB

Community Service Volunteers (Scotland)
236, Clyde Street,
Glasgow G1 4JH

Disabled Living Foundation
380-384 Harrow Road
London W9 2HU

Disability Scotland
Princes House,
5, Shandwick Place
Edinburgh EH2 4RG

Down's Syndrome Association,
155 Mitcham Road,
London SW17 9PG

ENABLE:(formerly Scottish Society for Mental Handicap)
6th Floor
7, Buchanan Street
Glasgow G1 3HL

Health Education Authority
78, New Oxford Street
London WC1

International League of Societies for Persons with Mental
  Handicap
248 Avenue Louise - bte 17
B - 1050 Brussels
Belgium

Lisieux Hall Publications
Whittle-le-Woods,
Chorley,
Lancashire PR6 7DX

King's Fund Centre
126, Albert Street
London NW1 7NF

MENCAP,
123, Golden Lane,
London, EC1Y 0RT

Mental Health Foundation
37, Mortimer Street
London W1N 7RJ

MIND: National Association for Mental Health
22, Harley Street
London W1N 2ED

National Children's Bureau
8, Wakley Street
London EC1V 7QE

National Citizen Advocacy
2 St. Paul's Road
London N1 2QR

National Council for Voluntary Organisations
Regent's Wharf,
8, All Saints Street,
London N1 9RL

National Development Team,
St. Peter's Court,
8, Trumpet Street,
Manchester M1 5LW

People First
Instrument House
207-215 King's Cross Road
London WC1X 9DB

Royal Association for Disability and Rehabilitation (RADAR)
25, Mortimer Street,
London W1N 8AB

RNIB Information Service on Multiple Disability
224, Great Portland Street
London W1N 6AA

Scottish Community Education Council,
9, Haymarket Terrace,
Edinburgh.

Scottish Council of Voluntary Organisations
18/19 Claremont Crescent,
Edinburgh EH7 4QD

Scottish Downs Syndrome Association
158/160 Balgreen Road
Edinburgh

Scottish Health Education Authority
Woodburn House,
Canaan Lane
Edinburgh EH10 4SG

SKILL: National Bureau of Students with Disabilities
336 Brixton Road
London SW9 7AA

SCOPE (formerly Spastics Society)
12, Park Crescent
London W1N 4EQ

Understanding Disability Educational Trust,
Weydon Lane,
Farnham,
Surrey GU9 8UG

Values into Action (VIA)
Oxford House
Derbyshire Street
London E2 6HG

VIA Publications
5, Kentings,
Comberton,
Cambs CB3 7DT

Volunteer Centre, U.K.,
Carriage Row, 183,
Eversholt Street,
London NW11 1BU.